changingchurch
for a changingworld

Fresh ways of being church
in a Methodist context

Contributions by
Martyn Atkins,
Tom Stuckey and
Martin Wellings

fresh expressions

The **Methodist** Church

Much of the material in this book was originally
written for a report to Methodist Conference that
has not been presented to Conference (2007)
because of lack of business time. Some material
was commissioned for this book and some written
in the transition.

Design & production: Methodist Church
Communication Office

ISBN 978-1-85852-335-4

Contents

Foreword

The Methodist people are no strangers to the idea of a changing church. Methodism was born from a passionate desire to see the gospel of Jesus Christ connect again with ordinary people in these islands and, indeed, all over the world. From the days of the Wesleys onwards that has meant God bringing to birth in every generation and culture fresh ways of being church.

In a time of great cultural change, this is happening once again and Methodists are at the forefront of being ready to change. When I was first invited to take up post as team leader of the Fresh Expressions initiative, I was delighted to learn that the whole adventure was to be a partnership between the Church of England and the Methodist Church – a practical outworking of our common commitment to the Covenant.

Over the last three years it's been my privilege to travel to almost every part of Britain and discover and learn about fresh ways of being church which are coming about as God's people listen again to the way the world is changing. We are realising, little by little, that it is no longer enough to invite people to join us in the church as we know it. It is no longer enough to change and adapt the church as we know it so as to be welcoming and accessible to those who do not know Christ. We need to learn again to go to where people are – on the other side of the street or the other side of the culture – first to listen, then to serve, then to discover ways of sharing faith and making disciples and then to develop communities which can grow to maturity as part of one body of Christ.

This is not an easy calling and I have been deeply moved to meet and talk with many Methodists who are determined to make this journey in the power and grace that God supplies. They have to be people with a strong sense of calling, the courage to admit that some things are not working, the imagination to think outside the box of the current church and the endurance to pursue new visions despite significant cost. The church at this time needs to cherish these pioneers. Whenever you meet someone with these gifts, take care to encourage them: they are a vital part of our community at the present time.

This booklet shares just some of the stories which are emerging across the Connexion as God's people step out in faith to develop fresh ways of church. It is suitable for those coming new to the subject and provides a basic explanation of fresh expressions of church and why they are needed. But there is also stronger meat here with challenging and helpful reflection from a theological and historical perspective.

There is much still to learn about how we develop these fresh expressions of church to their full potential but enough evidence already to show that we are beginning to see not just fresh green shoots here and there but a significant harvest for the kingdom of God. There is an urgent need now to provide training for the whole people of God in these ministries and that too is beginning to be set in place in many parts of the country. And there is a need in the Methodist Church as in the Church of England to reflect on what policy and structural changes will be needed to ensure that these fresh expressions of church are held in a connexion with the wider body of Christ to ensure that both learn from and give to each other. That in itself is a broad agenda and one which will need wisdom and grace in the coming years. You will find some of those questions raised in the pages that follow, but not yet answered: please help us as we seek together to encourage and enable all that is happening.

It has been my privilege for over a decade to work closely with the Methodist Church in training for ministry and encouraging mission. In that time I have come to appreciate and to give thanks for all that the Methodist Church represents in its own tradition and calling and I have learned much to enrich my own discipleship from Methodist friends and colleagues. The challenges and questions we face are significant but God's love and grace are more than sufficient for the task. I commend this book and the stories and wisdom it contains most warmly.

The Revd Dr Steven Croft
Archbishops' Missioner and Team Leader of Fresh Expressions

Introduction

This book contains three articles:

- Mission-shaped Thinking by Martyn Atkins pp 22-28

- An Historical Retrospective by Martin Wellings pp 30-33

- The Time is Short by Tom Stuckey pp 84-90

These can be read on their own but also provide essential background material for people wishing to understand the background and context of fresh expressions of church and the Fresh Expressions initiative within the Methodist Church of the early twenty-first century.

If you are using this book in a study group you might get a member of the group to read one of these articles and lead the group through it.

[1] *Called to Love and Praise*, Methodist Conference 1999

'In recent decades the world has undergone vast changes. In Britain and most of Western Europe, the churches are part of fast-changing, pluralist societies.' [1]

Taking advantage of these changes may disturb the comfort of some but they also provide the Church with great opportunities. Methodists need to remember that we emerged as a fresh expression of church in the eighteenth century and were led by the rule bending (breaking) John Wesley.

We cannot control the changes taking place in society in general, as always God calls the Church to be an agency of his mission called to live and witness in ways that make the good news of Jesus relevant to all. To some the most discomforting change in society is the growth of diversity. To others this change is welcome. For a church that has tended to standardize ways of doing things, and styles of worship and learning, this brings a challenge to reflect on how we do worship, what we teach and how we teach it.

Attendance and membership have been declining for nearly a century, as a percentage of the population for over 150 years. This trend is likely to continue for some time, but there are signs of growth and hope. For each of the last three years, the Methodist Church has made more new members than it made the year before. For each of the last five years more fresh expressions have started than the previous year.

In April 2007, there were 143 Methodist fresh expressions of church registered with the Fresh Expressions database.[2] This does not include those that are ecumenical expressions.

- There are 5063 adults and 2243 children involved in these.

- Children are 31% of the total.

- 39 define themselves as rural, 43 as suburban and 59 as urban.

- Fresh expressions are registered from almost all Methodist districts.

If the Church of England statistical returns[3] figures are mirrored in the Methodist Church the registered fresh expressions are only a small proportion of the total.

God made a world with seasons, a world with death and birth, and saved us through a Jesus who died and rose from the dead. The Church must embrace death if it is to have hope in resurrection. *'As it was in the beginning, is now, and ever shall be'*

was never meant to refer to the Church! Fresh Expressions bears witness to the growth of new ways of being church. We see numerous signs of a new springtime in the Church. The stories in this book tell of churches starting from scratch, churches with a majority of people under 40 years old, new churches in the centres of cities where we have closed old churches, and churches that have been resurrected or transformed.

In fresh expressions of church we find some of the traditional boundaries of the Church blurred. These fresh ways of being church challenge institutional wineskins designed for another age. They ask, 'Why do we do it this way?' and 'Why not try this?' Sometimes the new wine threatens to break out. Yet to take another biblical picture, the new growth is still growth on the vine of Christ, still rooted in his gospel, still attached to the rest of the vine, still in need of the sap of the Holy Spirit, still called to bear the same fruit.

Mission is carried out by all parts of the Church; it is not the preserve of fresh expressions. Maintaining what we have inherited and developing the new need not be mutually exclusive

[2] From the Fresh Expressions on line database at www.freshexpressions.org.uk on April 16th 2007. In all denominations there were 637 fresh expressions registered involving over 40,000 people including more than 13,000 children.

[3] The Church of England Parish Return statistics data gathered in October 2006 give figures of over 200,000 people involved in Anglican fresh expressions – only 22,000 are registered with Fresh Expressions.

activities. It is 'the Church that is' who will pray, and pay, for most of the fresh expressions as they emerge. Fresh expressions of church are marked by diversity, demographic, geographic, cultural, theological and ecclesiological. Fresh expressions of church are being developed by those from across the spectrum of preferred theology and tradition, 'charismatic', 'evangelical' 'sacramental', 'catholic', 'middle of the road' and 'radical'. Indeed it is one of the wonders of God's grace that some fresh expressions can do all of these at the same time! As diversity of expression increases we will need to know what holds us together. What is it that makes a fresh expression 'Methodist'? What does it mean to be in 'connexion'? As fresh expressions grow older, questions will arise about how they can become equal partners, paying their way and with their own governing structures. There will also be questions about keeping the expression fresh.

The development of fresh expressions is evidence of God at work. They are signs that give hope for the future. We are convinced that this hope is based on God's grace, mercy and love, not on any human systems and remedies.

The Church is primarily an agent of God's mission for the coming of His Kingdom. God is continually renewing his Church for this purpose. There are clear signs of the freshness of God's Spirit at work. The Spirit is both refreshing the old and bringing into being things of God's Kingdom that are completely new. We live in exciting times! We will tell something of this refreshing as well as examining the challenges this move of God's Spirit sets us.

The creativity of the Holy Spirit brings fresh expressions of church into existence and renews existing churches. God has brought such expressions of church into being throughout the history of the Church and throughout the world. As the gospel and cultures interact, communities of faith come into being. These communities live the gospel of Jesus in ways appropriate to their culture. It has been so from the beginning. It is so today within the churches of Britain and particularly within the Methodist Church.

We have not set out to reproduce in detail material found elsewhere. In particular, we would refer the reader to the Anglican report *Mission-shaped Church* (Church House Publishing).[4] The Methodist report *Time to Talk of God*, which we would recommend, also covers some areas of the changes in British society. *Called to Love and Praise* placed the nature of the Church in the context of God's mission. At the end of this book an appendix lists some of the responses of Methodist Conference, which have addressed changes in British society.

The development of fresh ways of being church for the changing world will naturally challenge our established ways of doing things. It is not our intention to provide an ecclesiological explanation or a fully worked out theology, but to present some of what is happening and the questions raised by this. We hope that a working party will be set up by Conference to encourage and monitor developments arising from the priority *'Encouraging fresh ways of being Church'*.

The illustrative stories of fresh expressions from around the country are only a sample of more than 150 Methodist fresh expressions known to us. We believe there are many more not known to us. Each of the stories has been written by someone who knows the fresh expression or is part of it. We have not sought to change their words or style. You may know of other fresh expressions that would usefully illustrate the matters addressed in this book. If you do, and are using the book as part of a group study or discussion, you will be able to bring the riches of the fresh expressions you know of to your discussions.[5]

The Fresh Expressions initiative is a partnership between the Church of England and the Methodist Church. In Scotland and Wales this partnership takes on a different flavour because the Church in Wales and the Episcopal Church of Scotland are not presently full partners with the initiative while the Methodist Church in both Scotland and Wales is.

[4] It is not our intention to repeat material already published in *Mission-shaped Church*. Readers are recommended to buy the printed version or download the report. See Resources appendix for details.

[5] Fresh Expressions has an on-line registry of fresh expressions. If you are part of a fresh expression which is not registered you can help other people by sharing your existence. www.freshexpressions.org.uk and click on 'Directory'.

'This key Anglican report [*Mission-shaped Church*] was developed by a working group which included Methodism's Evangelism and Church Planting Secretary. It is helpful for its analysis of contemporary culture and for its considered reflections on a variety of fresh expressions of church, and how some of the experiments have worked out. It explores theology and methodologies for a 'missionary church', and reminds us of the key values of such a church: that it is focussed on God the Trinity; that it is incarnational; that it is transformational; that it makes disciples; and that it is relational.'

Time to Talk of God, Methodist Publishing House, Peterborough, 1999. p.95

Fresh Expressions has published two DVDs of stories of fresh expressions of church and other materials that would be useful to any church exploring fresh ways of being church. More details of these are in the Resources appendix.

EXPRESSIONS: THE DVD 2
CHANGING CHURCH IN EVERY PLACE

Somewhere Else

Barbara Glasson

When the Methodist Church closed the Central Hall in the centre of Liverpool, some felt it to be like a withdrawal from the city. However, 12 years on something new is happening in the city centre. People who had once moved away are returning and the Methodist Church is determined to greet them. In a prophetic move, the church released the Revd Barbara Glasson to a street ministry, talking, and most importantly listening, to people in the centre of Liverpool.

In response to what Barbara heard, Somewhere Else was established; a community church with a difference. The congregation gathers around bread making three times a week and as people make their bread, they share their stories. Amazingly, whilst people wanted to share their stories they also felt moved to pray and read the Bible together. In this way, a community was born and now a group gathers on a Sunday to participate in worship with one another.

A typical mid-week gathering follows a simple pattern: first, people come together to make bread and share their stories. This is followed by an invitation to move into a more meditative space. In this reflective atmosphere, those gathered can listen to the rhythms of the city, each other's thoughts and the voice of God in their midst. It is through this that Somewhere Else provides a place of sanctuary from the pressures of life.

Somewhere Else may not be the project or the place for you but God might just have another 'somewhere else' for you. As Barbara comments, 'God is ahead of us to be discovered and sometimes that's despite our best plans.

Barbara has written of Somewhere Else in her book *Mixed-up Blessing* Somewhere Else is featured on 'Expressions - the DVD' (see the Resources appendix)

Devotion

James Church

The Devotion youth project is based in Marlborough, Wiltshire. It draws together several denominations, from Anglicans and Methodists to members of the United Reformed Church. In November 2002, the project started when Christchurch (Methodist/URC) appointed a full time youth worker, Dan Collins, to meet the needs of growing numbers of young people within its congregation.

Since November 2002, the Devotion youth project has developed its own identity. It works in partnership with other churches, local schools, and the youth development service to provide for both the social and spiritual needs of young people. In developing Devotion a number of schools and community work projects have been pursued including detached youth work, mentoring, DJ workshops, youth band workshops, an indoor skate park, trips, festivals, and residentials.

'It is great to see that Devotion is responding to the needs of the community', Dan Collins writes. 'Mission is at the heart of Devotion', which seeks to present 'the gospel in an authentic, genuine and culturally relevant way'. The main focus for Devotion remains Sunday evenings. These follow a monthly pattern, Café Devotion, the Devotion Youth Service, and peer focused Cell Groups.

On the first Sunday of the month, young people gather for Café Devotion. This event has a social focus and provides a way-in for young people who may be coming to church for the first time. On the second and fourth Sundays, they have small peer focused Cell Groups. These are Bible based discussion and discipleship groups. The third Sunday of the month is the Devotion Youth Service. This is led by young people for young people and involves a mixture of songs, stories imagery, ritual, and prayer.

In a medium sized rural town the gospel is flourishing thanks to the Devotion youth project, which touches the lives of over a hundred young people. Dan Collins and the Devotion team have been successful at reaching out to young people who have never been to church in their lives and sharing with them the knowledge and love of the Lord Jesus. I hope you will join with me in praying for God's continued blessing on the Devotion youth project.

Questions

Look at the piece on Somewhere Else on Expressions:
the DVD.

- **As you watch ask, 'What are the 'values' of this church?'**

Read the story of Devotion together.

- **What values underlie this fresh expression?**

The development of fresh expressions of church bring
a challenge to reflect on how we do worship, what
we teach and how we teach it as well as how we
do mission. Review how your church does these.
Review both the 'why' and the 'how'

- **What challenges do you face?**

- **Do you see signs of new life in your church
and circuit? If so what?**

Bible Study

- Reflect on Matthew 9:16-17

- What does this say to you
  in your present context?

- What is the significance of
  the word 'both' in verse 17

'fresh expressions' and 'Fresh Expressions'

We are using the term 'fresh expressions' – all lower case, no capitals – to refer to fresh expressions of church – local initiatives that explore different or new ways of being church as described in 'What is a fresh expression'.

If the words are capitalised they refer to the Fresh Expressions initiative.

Fresh Expressions was initially an initiative of the Archbishop of Canterbury, Rowan Williams. The Methodist Church, being in a covenant relationship with the Church of England, became a partner in the Fresh Expressions initiative as a focus of the Covenant's mission emphasis. The involvement of the Methodist Church in Fresh Expressions is also a response to the Connexional priorities adopted by Conference in 2004, and in particular the priority 'Encouraging fresh ways of being Church'.

Fresh Expressions began in September 2004 with the appointment of team leader Revd Dr Steven Croft. Pete Pillinger was appointed to the Connexional Team and seconded to Fresh Expressions in September 2005. Andrew Roberts, another Methodist minister, was appointed half time to the Fresh Expressions core team in 2006. Two other core team members, Ben Clymo and Rachel Matthews, currently attend Methodist churches.

OUR CALLING

SERVICE - The Church exists to be a good neighbour to people in need and to challenge injustice
What are our plans and targets for improving our community involvement over the next year?

LEARNING & CARING - The Church exists to help people to grow and learn as Christians, through mutual support and care
What are our plans and targets for developing our life together over the next year?

EVANGELISM - The Church exists to make more followers of Jesus Christ
What are our plans and targets for making more followers of Jesus Christ over the next year?

WORSHIP - The Church exists to increase awareness of God's presence and to celebrate God's love
What are our plans and targets for improving our worship over the next year?

www.methodistchurch.org.uk

Note the order the points of *Our Calling* are given. This is different to the normal order of Worship, Learning & Caring, Service and Evangelism. This reordering is deliberate. As normally stated the order is not meant to be one of importance, nor is it in our ordering.

In observing the development of fresh expressions of church, Fresh Expressions has noted that fresh expressions do not often start with a new worshipping community. More often they start with a group of people serving God and the world in loving service. This loving service often creates communities who become disciples of Jesus and develop their own worship life. The order in which we have given the four parts of *Our Calling* reflect this observation.

What is a 'fresh expression of church'?

[6] Dearborn, Tim, *Beyond Duty: a passion for Christ, a heart for mission*, MARC, 1998.

[7] We have not tried to differentiate between the Anglican and Methodist terminology. They are both coined to express the need for a changing church for a changing world. The Methodist Church became part of the Fresh Expressions initiative as part of its response to its own priorities.

[8] Readers are pointed to the Methodist report (Methodist Conference 1999) *Called to Love and Praise* for a study of 'church' in a Methodist context.

[9] Research from Christian Research, the Sheffield Centre and other sources show that approximately 10% of the British population are church members. About 30% attend church occasionally. In the last Census over 70% of the population described themselves as Christian.

Before we can ask what is a 'fresh expression of church' we need to know what church is. *Called to Love and Praise* tells us that *'The Church ... derives its very existence and purpose from God's reign and mission'*. Martyn Atkins, in his article below, has stressed the primary importance of the *Missio Dei – the Mission of God. 'It's not the Church of God which has a mission in the world but the God of mission who has a church in the world.'* [6]

This description of the purpose of the Church gives us one way of defining 'church'. *Our Calling* is another. The Church is called to service and evangelism – which are together, broadly, 'mission' as well as to worship which is the natural response of all people to the presence of God, and to express our discipleship in learning and caring. We can use the *Our Calling* statement as a 'litmus paper' for all churches, not just fresh expressions.

We might also use other models. *Our Calling* speaks of what we do, the creeds speak of what the Church is, 'one, holy, catholic and apostolic'. These are explored further in the section on a 'mixed economy' church.

It is no accident that the terms 'fresh ways of being church' and 'fresh expressions' came into being. We talk of 'fresh' rather than 'new' because there are fresh expressions based on ancient traditions such as monastic ideals – and these are far from new. We talk of 'fresh' because some are transformed 'traditional' expressions of church not new ones.

We talk of 'expressions of church', a term coined in *Mission-shaped Church*, and 'ways of being Church', the term used in the Methodist Priorities[7] because there are many ways in which disciples of Jesus can express his ministry in the world; many ways to worship, learn and care, serve and evangelise; many ways to be one, holy, catholic and apostolic. We have not sought to define 'church' except to use the term for much more than Sunday gatherings of Christians to worship God.[8]

Existing modes of church life touch about one third of the British population.[9] About ten per cent of the population are members of churches. It is clear that church as it is cannot reach all of a nation marked by growing cultural diversity. There is no call to replace what we presently do with something else. Rather there is a call to make room for expressions of church to arise in the communities that we do not at present reach. We therefore need to recognise that:

'A fresh expression of church is intended as a community or congregation which is, or has the potential to become, a church in its own right. It is not intended to be a half way house or stepping stone for someone joining a Sunday morning congregation.' [10]

There can be no watertight fresh expressions 'box' - however lack of definition leads to the phrase being used in ways that can make it meaningless. In response to numerous questions, Fresh Expressions[11] has developed a working definition of what a fresh expression of church is.

A fresh expression is a form of church for our changing culture established primarily for the benefit of people who are not yet members of any church.
- **It will come into being through principles of listening, service, incarnational mission and making disciples.**
- **It will have the potential to become a mature expression of church shaped by the gospel and the enduring marks of the church and for its cultural context.**

BUT
It is clear that the refreshing power of God is not just establishing fresh expressions of church. There is clear evidence of imagination running riot within existing churches. There are fresh expressions of church and fresh expressions of what we already do – and the boundaries are not clear.

'[The Bible's] varying pictures and models of the Church suggest that diversity, development, and new responses to changing situations and context are the norm. But in all situations, the underlying truth of the Church's nature and purpose remains the same: by its life and witness the Church points towards, and by sharing and worship it anticipates, and through its mission it is an instrument of the ultimate reality of the Kingdom of God, actualised in Jesus Christ.'
Called to Love and Praise 2.3.19

[10] http://www.freshexpressions.org.uk/section.asp?id=25 (2006)

[11] http://www.freshexpressions.org.uk/section.asp?id=1768 (2006)

THE SANCTUARY
SW1
CITY OF WESTMINSTER

The Sanctuary

James Church

At Methodist Central Hall, Westminster, on Thursday evenings a community of twenty and thirty year olds meet to explore what it means to be a Christian living, working or studying in central London. It has grown from four members to about 60 with over 100 gathering at its first anniversary; a fantastic testimony to the lives it has touched.

The Sanctuary meets in a number of formats; the main worship happens bi-weekly and begins with forty-five minutes of coffee, cookies and good conversation. It follows a contemporary, albeit, conventional style of service with worship, word, and prayer ministry offered towards the end of the evening. On the alternate weeks people meet for Sanctuary Re:mixed, a creative worship evening which is whatever members makes it. Recently, this has involved group discussions, interviews, testimonies, nooma™ video reflections, and various styles of worship.

In addition to these services, the community has its own gospel choir, a creativity evening called The Canvas, small discipleship groups, and offers support to a project working with the homeless in the City of Westminster. In the summer of 2007, The Sanctuary is going to Greenbelt Christian festival and planning a trip to Taizé ecumenical community.

Speaking to members at The Sanctuary, they are thankful for this place to belong to in London, for the opportunity to reflect, to ask questions about God, and to grow in discipleship. Jonathan Green, The Sanctuary's founding pastor, thanks God for the community saying, 'it is humbling that God keeps gracing us with his presence, that people keep coming along and giving testimony to the fact that God is involved here in the community'.

It is great hearing about the wonderful things God is doing through The Sanctuary; people making new friends, discovering Jesus, growing in faith and developing their gifts. More information about The Sanctuary can be found online at www.sanctuary-westminster.org

The Terminus Initiative

Joy Adams

A Methodist church on an estate in Sheffield, in 2000, went onto the streets with a questionnaire asking their neighbours what mattered to them and what the church could do to help. 'The majority of people didn't recognise that the church could play a role and were surprised at the question,' recalls Joy Adams, a Methodist minister on the Lowedges estate, which has a reputation for anti-social behaviour and drugs.

The most pressing local needs included a drop-in centre for the elderly and youth activities. The church realised that any response would need to come from all the local churches and formed an ecumenical partnership.

'From the start we worked in partnership with the different agencies on the estate,' says Joy. 'We said right at the start we are four churches motivated by God's love.'

The churches leased a local shop and set up The Terminus Café. It is self-financing, includes a charity shop, and opens three days a week to around 60 visitors a day, and one evening a week for young people. Café staff open and close the day with prayer which is visible through the window. Now there is a prayer request board and one-to-one prayer is available.

The café's Christian remit is made clear by a monthly service, 'Worship at The Terminus' at 4.30 on a Thursday afternoon. When the idea of the service was first mooted it was greeted with 'shock', Joy says. Bible study groups happen in series of four or five weeks at varying times and venues to suit the differing needs of local residents.

Volunteers from across the churches and community now staff the café and The Terminus initiative has been created to cover the café, an asylum seekers befriending service and a credit union. The maisonette above the café, The Terminus Upper Rooms, houses offices for The Terminus Initiative and the Primary Care Trust Community Health Worker and is ,a venue for meetings.

When assessors for the Duke of York Community Awards asked The Terminus' neighbours for their opinion, the Sikh shopkeeper next door but one replied, 'These are the best neighbours I've ever had and I feel safest when the café is open.'

> 'What we have to be involved in is not the revival of the Church or the reform of the Church. It has to be nothing less than what Paul and the Fathers of the Council of Jerusalem were involved in for their time - the refounding of the Catholic Church for our age.'
>
> Vincent Donovan, analysing the task of reaching western culture. *Christianity Rediscovered*, (p. vii)

Questions

Look at the *Our Calling* panel above, p.15. The questions on each of the four quadrants are from the Methodist website.

- **Can any or all of these be realised by planning a fresh expression of church?**

Reflect on the way we have re-ordered the four parts of *Our Calling*:

- **Does this change your understanding of how *Our Calling* relates to your church and its priorities?**

Make a list of the fresh expressions you know of in your circuit/district/area.

- **What do you know about them?**
- **How did they start?**
- **Who leads them?**
- **Which community are they based in?**

Bible Study

Read (in The Message if possible)

Genesis 1:1-31
Isaiah 43:15-19
Revelation 2:1-5

- What do these passages say to you about the nature of God?
- From what you have learned of the nature of God – how is this reflected in the 'missio Dei' – the mission of God?

- If the Church is an agent of the 'missio Dei', how can this be reflected in the Church?
- How can this be reflected in your church?
- Do the stories of The Sanctuary and The Terminus reflect in any way what you have learned from the Bible passages?
- In the New Testament the Church is likened to salt, light, a vineyard, a body, the bride of Christ. What other descriptions do you know?
- What do these tell you of God and the 'missio Dei'?

Understanding Our Context

Two articles from Methodist scholars to prompt your thinking and for further reading.

Mission-shaped Thinking

Martyn Atkins

An Historical Retrospective

Martin Wellings

Fresh ways of being church in a Methodist context

Mission-shaped Thinking

Martyn Atkins

That the Christian Church is primarily 'mission-shaped' is one of the key theological rediscoveries of our times. This reawakening as to the mission shapedness of church is today resulting in an explosion of wonderful variety and creativity which is currently identified by the phrase 'fresh expressions of church'. This short article focuses mainly on the first assertion, that the essential nature and purpose of the Christian Church is missional, then contends that fresh expressions are a perfectly normal and expected outcome of church, understood as the agent of the mission of God.

In the beginning... God

Having stated that the focus is on church it may seem odd to suggest that that is the wrong starting point. But it is. Paradoxically, even when dealing with material about the nature of the church you can't properly begin at that point. As two Catholic writers recently put it, 'One of the most important things Christians need to know about the church is that *the church is not of ultimate importance.*'[12] This is not to suggest that the church is unimportant, quite the reverse, but it is to set church in a proper theological context.

Where then does mission-shaped thinking about church, properly begin? It begins with God, with theology, reflection upon and talk about God. Just as we cannot look at our own eyes without a mirror for reflection, so the church is unable to see itself for what it is without seeing itself via something else. Mission-shaped thinking suggests that the 'something else' is the God of mission. And not just any god, but the God revealed in the Christian Scriptures, God experienced and understood in terms of Father, Son and Holy Spirit.

[12] S Bevans and R Schroeder, *Constants in Context: a theology of mission for today*, Orbis, 2004, p7.

Without rejecting the complexities of Scripture in terms of text, type, genre, form, and the like - there lies in mission, shaped thinking a conviction that the meta-story of Scripture can be discerned and bears witness to the fundamental character of God as missionary and evangelist. The Old Testament declares God to be creator of all things, one grieved at the spoiling of creation, but one who, even as humankind signs its own death warrant in Eden, is working for the restoration of everything and everyone. God's redemptive plans are worked out through patriarchs and prophets, matriarchs and messengers, covenants and torah, signs and symbols. The means are varied and costly, but the overall aim, God's mission, is plain. In the fullness of time God, Father Son and Holy Spirit conspire again and a crucial phase of the divine mission takes shape. Christ Jesus, God incarnate, God 'self-sent' as it were, accomplishes the missionary task of redeeming all humanity, all creation. God in Christ does what neither the cosmos nor humankind can do for itself: dying he destroys our death and rising he restores our life.

The Son embodies the nature and mission of God.

But that is not the end. As fledgling communities of those believing in Jesus the Christ are born, God again takes the initiative, and comes revealed as Holy Spirit - a missionary self-sending God in action again. The Holy Spirit is a major figure and theme in mission-shaped church thinking. The Methodist tradition has a rich view of the Holy Spirit. John Wesley spoke about and relied upon the Holy Spirit in terms of what he called prevenient grace. Put simply, this marvellous theme acknowledged God's 'going beforeness' into every context and situation. When Christians declared their faith to unbelievers, when missionaries entered uncharted territories, of one thing Christians could be sure: God the Holy Spirit had 'gone before', preparing a way, already 'there', in the world. Inside *and* outside the Church then, the Spirit comes, making bold, leading outwards, going before, preparing the way 'to Jerusalem, Samaria and to the ends of the earth.' As F.F. Bruce used to say about the book of Acts, 'it is as if God drops a pebble into the pool of human history, and we watch the ripples'.

Nor is God's missionary nature limited to the revelation in Scripture. Through Christian history, today, all around the world, God is on a mission of redemption and restoration. In the words of the late John V Taylor in that still great book *The Go-Between God*,[13] 'The Holy Trinity have put together a rescue package', and what we call 'church' is, by divine design, intrinsic to the package. God – Father, Son and Spirit – is, first to last, a missionary evangelistic God, and this conviction is usually referred to by the shorthand phrase, *missio Dei*, literally meaning 'The mission of God' or 'God's mission'.

Seek first God's Kingdom...

If Christian mission proceeds from the revealed nature of the Trinity, then the *focus* and *goal* of mission is shaped by the perceived nature of God's Kingdom. 'The Kingdom or Reign of God represents the overriding missional perspective of the New Testament'.[14] The tapestry which is God's Kingdom cannot be even sketched out here, suffice it to say that a Kingdom focus offers to those sharing in God's mission a rich and varied mission to participate in. Sharing with God in bringing in the Kingdom involves every facet of human life, the whole of life, in all creation. 'Thy Kingdom come' may trip off the tongue easily enough, but it is a goal that fills lives and it is the ultimate

purpose of the Church. Such a calling rescues us from making God's mission too small, or narrow. Or, when we do fall into that trap, challenges us. Mission cannot properly be understood in terms of building up the 'interior' life of the Church, or perpetuating the internal traditions of local churches. Yet here is one of the mysteries: although the Kingdom is not to be confused with the life of the Church, participating in God's mission and pursuing the Kingdom inevitably results in Christian communities being formed and thereby 'church' appears naturally. Kingdom and church are therefore intrinsically connected and consequently getting a right understanding of the connection is vital. Mission-shaped thinking considers this happens when the Church is set free for the Kingdom of God.

Then the Church....

Where have we got to? The Church derives its being from the missionary God and is created and shaped to share in the *missio Dei* the goal of which is the coming of God's Kingdom. To put it more technically, ecclesiology derives from missiology which itself derives from theology - from the nature of God, Father, Son and Holy Spirit. David Bosch writes, 'The classical doctrine of the

[13] John V Taylor, *The Go-Between God: The Holy Spirit and the Christian Mission*, SCM Press, 1972

[14] Donald E Messer, *A Conspiracy of Goodness: Contemporary Images of Christian Mission*, Abingdon Press, 1992, p.39.

missio Dei as God the Father sending the Son, and God the Father and the Son sending the Spirit was expanded to include yet another 'movement': Father, Son and Holy Spirit sending the Church into the world.'[15] In this way the Christian Church finds its proper place in the scheme of things. It derives its life, nature, mission and ministry – in short its 'shape' - from the Christian Godhead. Whatever God is perceived to be like the Church (if it is faithful and true) will be like. 'As the Father sent me' says Jesus, 'so I send you.'[16] If God is supreme missionary, going before, searching out, inviting and receiving in, abiding with, then these characteristics will be those of the Church of this God. If God is experienced as self giving, and urging and bringing *shalom*, then so will the Church be, and so on. As Paul Stevens (echoing Jurgen Moltmann and St Augustine) reminds us, the Church 'does not *have* a mission; it *is* mission. There is... one trinitarian people... that reflects the one God who is lover, beloved and love itself... one God who is sender, sent and sending.'[17] It is largely this understanding of church that is outlined in mission-shaped church literature and which under girds the energy and challenge of fresh expressions of church.

Fresh Expressions

Church understood in this way has ramifications. For example, whenever being missional is relegated or supplanted as the essential characteristic of church things are deemed to be awry and incomplete. It is no accident that the Pentecost event marks not only the 'birthday' of the Church but also the 'birthday' of the Christian mission. So Church defined by the *missio Dei* never finds its true centre by focusing inwards on itself. Whenever preoccupation with its own survival takes centre stage then the Church has lost sight of its raison d'etre and ceased to live harmoniously with its very life-force. As Lesslie Newbigin commented, 'When the Church ceases to be a mission... it ceases to have any rights to the titles by which she is adorned in the New Testament. [18]

Another key outcome of mission-shaped Church thinking is the inevitability of fresh expressions coming to be, of church being in a constant state of change. Why is this? A short answer is a) because God requires church to change in order to share in the *missio Dei* in many different cultural contexts, b) because the Christian Church is

[15] David J Bosch, *Transforming Mission: Paradigm Shifts in Theology of Mission*, Orbis, 1991, p.390.

[16] John 20:21.

[17] Paul R Stevens, *The Abolition of the Laity: Vocation, Work and Ministry in a Biblical Perspective*, Paternoster Press, 1999, p.5-6.

[18] Lesslie Newbigin, *The Household of God*, SCM Press, 1953, p.163.

incarnational by nature like Jesus Christ its Lord, and c) because it is impelled to change by the Holy Spirit of God who is a Spirit of mission. Consider for a moment, if Christianity – and church as the key visible expression of it - were not able to undergo profound changes Christianity would have withered on its first vine, rendering propagation impossible. 'Translatability'[19] is one of the great geniuses of Christianity and the fact that Christianity can take root in different soils and produce true Christian disciples around the world, down the centuries, and up into heaven is nothing short of miraculous. Given the nature of the Christian faith why should we be surprised at this? Taking its lead from its divine Lord an incarnational religion like Christianity is always going to be changing shape in order that the gospel can be authentically offered to each new generation, to each new cultural context, to each emerging social environment. If Christianity were unchanging, if it could not incarnate and communicate God's gospel news to each and every changing context, then how can it truly be the expression of Christ at all?

There are of course perennial debates about whether the changes the Church

undergoes are the right changes. The relationship of Christianity to its broad culture context is a complex and challenging balancing act. The Christian Church walks a fine line between simple capitulation to a prevailing culture, melting into it and losing its identity as God's prophetic sign to the world, while on the other hand resisting the temptation to withdraw from the world in ways which deny its true missional nature. In short, in relation to its cultural context church cannot opt out, but mustn't fall in.[20] In each great period of Christian history there have been fresh expressions of church. Some tend to be inculturated, deeply engaged in their broader cultural context, others call people out from 'the world' to form church. This is no accident, and we should expect various fresh expressions of 'engaged' and 'called out' church to emerge in our own changing cultural context as a natural consequence of the Church finding its primary identity and character in the *missio Dei*.

Christianity, then, changes – as do expressions of church as an intrinsic part of that process. New forms of church have accompanied every era of Christian mission and witness since the day of Pentecost, and as is pointed

[19] See Lamin Sanneh, *Translating the Message: Missionary impact on Culture*, Orbis, 1989.

[20] See Martyn D Atkins, *Preaching in a Cultural Context*, Foundery Press, 2001

out elsewhere in this book, Methodism was a potent fresh expression of its day. Fresh expressions then, are normative for a faith like Christianity: wonderful, but entirely normal. Fresh expressions signal the comforting reality that the missionary Spirit of God has not given up on us, that we in the Church today continue to be called to share in God's mission. But they also signal the challenging reality that in order to share in God's mission a greater variety of expressions of church are required than the recent past provides. Put sharply, if the *missio Dei* in any time and place cannot be pursued with the Church as it is, God raises up a new church for the purpose. Methodists, of all Christians, should understand this.

Of course the real challenge of mission-minded thinking about church is turning thinking into reality. It isn't easy. 'Church for church's sake' is a subtle temptation common to very many congregations today. Even when the rhetoric is missionary, outward and Kingdom oriented, church life lived-out often signals different priorities. It is a harsh and ironic reality that sheer investment over many years makes many church folk susceptible to automatically assuming that the routine

life and ministry of the local church *is* seeking the Kingdom, and keeping the 'show on the road' *is* sharing in the mission of God. It is precisely because this temptation is so common that the missionary nature of the Church requires to be rehearsed over and over again. One of the reasons I am enthusiastic about fresh expressions of church is that mission mindedness and shapedness is so often evident. Indeed one of the 'prompts' of the Spirit resulting in a 'fresh expression' is often a realisation that Jesus said he would build his Church, and told his followers to go and make disciples. One of the best energisers of inherited congregations I know is to prayerfully revisit the missionary nature of the Church and deliberately develop an authentic, contextually apt fresh expression of church. After all, making babies is more fun than making coffins!

Martyn Atkins is Principal of Cliff College and President of Conference 2007

Questions

- When have you experienced God 'going before' you, preparing away for you? (Prevenient Grace)

Look at the Lord's Prayer (probably the bit of the Bible most people know by heart),

- What do you imagine a world in which 'Your Kingdom' has come would be like? A world where God's will is done.

- What can you do to make our world more like this?

- More specifically, what can you do to make where you live more like this?

- Do you recognise your church to be a community/place where God's will is done and which is a sign of God's Kingdom?

- If 'yes' – what is the evidence for this?

- If 'no' – what can you do to make God's Kingdom come in your church?

Martyn writes that 'The relationship of Christianity to its broad cultural context is a complex and challenging balancing act.'

Identify areas in the life of your church where you feel the balance is wrong.

- Where might you challenge contemporary culture?

- Where might you be being challenged by contemporary culture?

An Historical Retrospective

Martin Wellings

The churches are gradually learning the language of 'fresh expressions', but the ideas underpinning the new phraseology are as old as the gospel itself. For the best part of two thousand years a blend of Spirit-led creativity, evangelistic necessity, cultural pressure and sheer restlessness has encouraged or compelled Christians to seek new ways of proclaiming and embodying the Good News of Jesus Christ.

We could claim that the Wesleys' Methodism was in itself a 'fresh expression' of the life and mission of the Church. In its commitment to evangelism, its quest for holiness and its emphasis on experience, the movement contrasted sharply with the attitudes and priorities of much of the contemporary Church. The practice of open-air evangelism ('field-preaching'), the use of lay men and women as preachers and the setting of new hymns to popular secular tunes scandalised staid contemporaries, but attracted sections of the population others had failed to reach. The evolving structures of the movement, with a system of mutually accountable discipleship groups and local lay leadership supervised by itinerant preachers answerable to the annual Conference, created a tight-knit

'Christianity itself has its origins as a fresh expression of Judaism and the New Testament canon demands that Christianity is continually refreshed by a return to sources but expresses itself differently in different contexts.'

Professor James Dunn of Durham University, a Methodist local preacher

'Connexion' able to deploy resources and respond to opportunities in the fast-changing society of late eighteenth and early nineteenth century England.

Methodist creativity continued after John Wesley's death, although two famous 'fresh expressions' which grew within Methodism eventually parted company with their parent body. In the first decades of the nineteenth century some Methodists borrowed the technique of 'camp meetings' – open-air gatherings for prayer and preaching – from the American frontier, where Methodism was growing rapidly. In revolutionary times Conference was nervous about large public meetings; the leaders of the new initiative were expelled, and 'Primitive Methodism' was born. Half a century later William and Catherine Booth left a Connexion unable to cope with their innovative but autocratic methods of evangelism and organisation; the result was the creation of the Salvation Army.

Mainstream Methodism remained committed to reaching a growing urban population with the gospel. One initiative was the 'Forward Movement' of the 1880s, which found expression in the building of the Central Halls. In architecture, style of worship, method of outreach, organisation and ethos the halls and the central missions were distinctive, and they certainly began as a conscious 'fresh expression' of Christian life and witness.

Other examples of 'fresh expressions' may be less well known but nonetheless significant. The nineteenth century saw phenomenal growth in Sunday schools, lay led and sometimes largely independent of their host church. Groups for women – 'sisterhoods', 'mothers' meetings' and 'bright hours' – also flourished in this period, acting as a midweek opportunity for worship and fellowship; the 'Pleasant Sunday Afternoon' and the Brotherhood Movement fulfilled a similar function for men. From the 1930s churches experimented with cinema services to reach new congregations. As slums were cleared and new towns constructed in the years around the Second World War, new churches were planted, often initially without buildings or in dual purpose premises. Groups like the Wesley Guild, the Cliff Fellowship and MAYC could become, in effect, new congregations with a particular style, appeal and clientele. In more recent times Sheffield has seen new forms of community under the umbrella of the Sheffield Inner City

Ecumenical Mission, pioneered by John Vincent.

At their best, church structures took outreach seriously. The Wesleyan Methodists, for instance, set up a Home Mission fund to promote evangelism and church-planting. Ministers were designated for service as evangelists; when the districts were given 'separated Chairs', these posts were often combined with a particular evangelistic role. Concern about church growth, however, did not always lead to innovation and fresh thinking. Sometimes there was a call for a return to the old ways, which were seen as more authentic and more effective. This was the burden of the 'Liverpool Minutes', adopted by the Conference of 1820 in response to a decline in membership (note too that the 'camp meeting' Methodists of the early 1800s deliberately harked back to the origins of Methodism by calling themselves 'Primitive Methodists'!).

History, then, does not teach easy lessons. 'Fresh expressions' can reinvigorate old structures, or can prove incompatible with them. The new wine of the eighteenth century revival burst the old wineskins of the existing denominations (although some proved remarkably resilient). The period of Methodism's most rapid growth – the half-century after John Wesley's death – was also the period of greatest division, as the movement splintered into more than half-a-dozen competing connexions. Methodism could not contain the Booths and it made life uncomfortable for Hugh Price Hughes, champion of the 'Forward Movement'. Innovation is no more assured of support than it is of success. Change is essential and inevitable, but it is seldom easy!

Successful innovation in one generation, moreover, could become a stereotype constraining the next, as a 'fresh expression' became a stale expression, commanding nostalgic loyalty in inverse proportion to its effectiveness. Arguably the patterns of the immensely successful late-Victorian and Edwardian chapel culture (which included plenty of new ideas and adaptation to changing conditions) became frozen in the twentieth century as generations taught and shaped by the young people of the 1910s looked back wistfully from the 1970s and 1980s to a world we had lost.

It is worth remembering that these historical instances of 'fresh expressions' did not always come about as totally new ideas. John Wesley was famously a borrower and adapter of other peoples' projects. He took up open-air preaching very reluctantly, at George Whitefield's insistence, and it is likely that Whitefield got the idea from Welsh revivalists. Wesley's 'societies' grew from the Oxford 'Holy Club', which in itself mirrored seventeenth century groups for nurturing spirituality. Likewise, Primitive Methodism took its inspiration from the Americans, albeit in modified form.

Good ideas, then, were passed around. The leaders of the eighteenth century revival corresponded across oceans and continents. Stories of what we would call 'best practice' circulated in manuscript and in printed journals (Wesley's famous Journal was composed for publication: it was not a private and personal diary). With the spread of literacy and the burgeoning of publications in the nineteenth century, creative innovations in one place could be reported, assessed and replicated elsewhere. Memoirs and biographies encouraged fresh thinking; experienced evangelists offered 'how

to' manuals on such topics as open-air speaking. This flow of encouragement continues today. Sharing stories, learning from other people's experience, drawing inspiration and guidance from fellow Christians of many traditions, locations and backgrounds are not only modern wisdom; they are all practices firmly rooted in the best of our heritage.

Martin Wellings is a Methodist minister and Secretary of the Northampton District

Further Reading

From the 'Exploring Methodism' series:-
* Barrie Tabraham, *The Making of Methodism* (Peterborough: Epworth, 1995).
* Geoffrey Milburn, *Primitive Methodism* (Peterborough: Epworth, 2002).
Also, two studies of early Methodism:
* Richard P. Heitzenrater, *Wesley and the People called Methodists* (Nashville: Abingdon, 1995).
* John Munsey Turner, *John Wesley. The Evangelical Revival and the Rise of Methodism in England* (Peterborough: Epworth, 2002).
And on the changes of the nineteenth century:
* Charles D. Cashdollar, *A Spiritual Home. Life in British and American Reformed Congregations, 1830-1915* (Pennsylvania State University Press, 2000).

Questions

- **What was new about the Wesleys' Methodism?**

- **What was a fresh way of expressing an old truth?**

- **What was familiar and traditional about the beliefs, practices and structures of the Methodist movement?**

Investigate the history of a church or congregation you know well.
- **How and why did it start?**

Try to find out about its successes and its failures, and the causes of each.
- **What lessons does the story of that church contain for you in your present situation?**

In your church what new 'traditions' have emerged in the last 10 years?
- **Why?**
- **What things which have been good to do in the past are no longer helpful?**
- **What changes would you like to make in the next year? The next five years?**

- **If the new hymns of early Methodism, set to secular tunes, scandalised the Wesleys' contemporaries, what scandalises our contemporaries today?**

- **If we want to learn from modern examples of 'best practice', where do we look?**

- **Where are the sources of inspiration and creativity for today's church? (Be as specific as you can!)**

World Church Perspectives

Christians in other parts of the world are used to developing church in cultures where Christianity has never been dominant. We have much to learn from our world church partners and our mission partners with them. The writings of Lesslie Newbigin,[21] Roland Allen[22] and others who have served the world church give indications about the principles needed if we are to encourage fresh expressions of church. Our world church in Britain mission partners come with their own Christian heritage that often challenges our own. We need to learn from both the past and from our sisters and brothers in other parts of the world as we respond to a movement of God's Spirit in our own age and place.

Among the Methodist churches of the United Kingdom are some who worship and express their life in Christ in other languages.

sri lanka

In recent years the Methodist Church of Sri Lanka has been growing at 5% p.a. It has planted not just a number of churches but even numbers of circuits. In the late 1980's the Church established a new order of evangelists. According to a former President of Conference of Sri Lanka this growth is primarily due to the order of evangelists.

cuba

The Methodist Church in Cuba has passed through hard times since the revolution which brought Fidel Casto to power. In recent years it has become one of the fastest growing Methodist churches in the world. People are starting 'missiones' and then the Church recognises the proven ministry they have exercised by ordaining them. The primary qualification they bring is not theoretical training or an exploration of vocation – it is a track record of having started a church from scratch! For those who have done this the Church offers support and training to enhance their proven abilities.

[21] C.F Newbigin, L, *The Gospel in a Pluralist Society*, SPCK, London, 1989

[22] Allen, Roland, *Missionary Methods – St Paul's or Ours?*, Eerdemans, Grand Rapids, 1962 (originally published 1927

Doncaster

In Doncaster a Farsi speaking congregation has grown among former Muslims from Persia.....

Colin Reasbeck

The first Iranians were baptised at the Hexthorpe Methodist Church at Easter 2002. At that stage they worshipped with the English congregation. When it became clear there was only partial understanding and the numbers were growing, it was decided they should leave halfway through the service for their own message, given through interpretation. Numbers grew until on occasion Iranians outnumbered English people. In July 2004 a separate Farsi language service was started after the English language service. A few have continued to attend the latter. Attendances at the Farsi language service peaked at around 120 in autumn 2004 and have since settled at around 70 people. Special speakers attract believers from other towns. A month ago the church was full with over 150 present. Many move out (to London or other cities) once they are given asylum. Some only came once or twice, others used the opportunity of spare time (not being allowed to work) of studying the Bible in midweek groups at the church and in house groups two or three times a week. Frankly, we have never experienced such hunger among English people. There are three identifying features of this congregation:

- all are Farsi speakers (including some Afghans),
- all are from a Muslim background,
- all are originally asylum seekers.

Why has this group developed? The only real explanation is God through his word and Spirit. We did not worry what motive brought people. There has been a warm welcome to the church which is open to newcomers. Although some may have just been wanting to bolster their asylum claim, we took the opportunity of teaching them the Scriptures. 'Faith comes by hearing the word of God.' (Romans 10:17) It was important they were taught and worshipped in their own language. It was recognised that dreams were important in their culture. Regular midweek Bible studies were held alongside Sunday worship. People were encouraged from the beginning to share their faith with others. The greatest challenges have been encouraging a new lifestyle and developing leaders. Five have begun to preach. Believers have

been baptised by immersion. We have helped with legal and housing problems. Receiving so many new-comers is costly in time and energy, and at times disturbing, but immensely rewarding.

The movement of Iranians to the Christian faith both in Iran and outside – in Europe, Australia and North America – has been described as the biggest movement of Muslims to the Christian faith since that in Indonesia in the 1960's. It has been a privilege to share in a small way in this. 'Why Iran?' we are often asked. It is clear God has his own agenda for this country which hits the headlines so often. As we show the Persian thread running through the Bible, from the King of Elam (Genesis 14) to Daniel, Cyrus and Esther, to the Elamites at Pentecost, a modern Iranian, who already feels that Islam was forced upon his country through Arab invaders and has probably left Iran because of Islam's recent record there, will quickly see that the Bible relates more to his country than ever the Koran did. There is also a small group of Afghan men who have become Christian believers, mainly through contact with the Farsi language group. Being

only eight out of over 200 Afghans in Doncaster, they do not have an easy time, but know much worse awaits them should they not be granted asylum. We also know of Chinese and French speaking African groups, not to mention many English speaking African Christians, in Doncaster – there are more than 70 language groups represented in our town. Does God, in his mercy, plan to revitalise the Church in England through such incomers? If so, we are blessed indeed.

Chinese Methodist Mission

Geoff Cornell

A nationwide group of Methodist churches speaking Cantonese and Mandarin is based at the Methodist church in Kings Cross, London. In collaboration with local churches and circuits, this 'super-circuit' has congregations in many parts of the country....

Although there has been a Chinese Methodist Mission in Britain for 40 years, the significant growth has occurred in the last 15. Under the leadership of Revd David Foo, a congregation moved to Kings Cross Methodist Church, where proximity to Chinatown, good transport links and an easier engagement with the student community produced a rapid increase. Quickly it grew to over 200 attending. An active church with strong evangelical zeal, it has an advice service for illegal immigrants and this year has begun a Mandarin service alongside the Cantonese one. From this a congregation was planted in Epsom Methodist Church and from these two have sprung congregations in Norwich, Gillingham, Hastings, Derby, Newcastle, Middlesborough and Exeter. In one sense these are not 'fresh expressions' in that the theology and style of worship is conservative, but in another sense,

with the planting of congregations within language groups, they undoubtedly are. Most of the planted churches have congregations in excess of 60 and these are the hub of wider fellowships such as those in restaurants for people working long hours there. Bible study at midnight is not the lot of the average Methodist minister! The Christian faith is finding a particular home in the hearts of Chinese migrants and adult baptisms, upon profession of faith, are regular. The mission field is inviting: there are 50,000 Chinese students in Britain and 50,000 illegal immigrants – as well as those who have settled in this country by other means.

The work is a partnership, properly led by the Chinese Mission itself. Preachers travel from London to Newcastle and other places – rather further than the average local preacher might anticipate. The ministry team consists of David Foo, KK Yap and John Yap (all ministers formerly serving in the Malaysian Methodist Church). Of the indigenous Chinese, Hazel Yu has just come to Epsom as a probationer minister and Lawrence Law is in pre-ordination training in Birmingham. There are a number of preachers, some of whom are accredited local preachers through overseas conferences, but others who have studied at the only Chinese language Christian training centre in Europe, COCM, based in Milton Keynes. In each town, there are partnerships between the Chinese congregations and the hosting Methodist church, which, in the more mature congregations at Kings Cross and Epsom has resulted in the pattern of two (or more) congregations but the one church council. The financing of the work is also a partnership between the congregations themselves; British Methodism (which has been generous in its grants) and the Hong Kong Methodist Church.

A feature of the Church in Britain today illustrated by the Chinese Mission is that growth is often found among migrant populations and working within a particular culture and language is particularly effective. But such work also throws up questions that are difficult even for a Church such as Methodism that is founded on itinerancy and seeks to be flexible in responding to mission opportunities. A crucial question is the relationship between emerging church and traditional church.

- As a movement gains strength when does it move out of a dependent relationship to the host church and into a proper partnership through assuming responsibilities such as property and finance?
- How can traditional church facilitate the development of indigenous leadership whilst not simply giving people carte blanche to do their own thing and thus encourage separation?
- How can these questions be engaged with when people are (literally) not speaking the same language and do not even have the same (Methodist and other) culture?

These are questions that underpin discussions about church council attendance, finding ways of training preachers who speak little English, and if you think Safeguarding is difficult in your church, try implementing it when people in the congregation are in the country illegally!

At present the Chinese Mission is a hybrid organisation – relating to local churches but also the wider mission outreach (a kind of super-circuit!); part of Methodism and seeking validation

within it yet with a distinctive agenda;
working within different Far Eastern
cultures and languages yet also aware
that the next generation will be English
speaking. It is exciting to be involved.
It requires care and tolerance on
all sides as we chart a necessarily
experimental way ahead. But I vaguely
remember the early Church sharing
some of these characteristics and
St Paul offering wise counsel as people
responded to similar workings of
the Spirit.

. . . .

Developing expressions of church that cross cultures always challenge the
established culture of the church. These expressions of church, which are fresh
to the United Kingdom, highlight issues and opportunities available to us as
we seek to develop fresh ways of being church to reach people of British cultures
that are different from church norms but do not originate from overseas.
We must not see them as exceptions because they are 'foreign' but be
ready to learn from the wider church, both overseas and in Britain.

Questions

- What lessons can we learn from our interaction with the world church?

- Could British Methodism follow the church in Cuba in ordaining those who have started churches?
  - What advantages/disadvantages might there be in this?

- How do we adapt British Methodism to take account of the world church in Britain – ethnic congregations like the Chinese and Farsi ones featured? How, for example, do we authorise ministry for those congregations?

Look at the questions raised by Geoff Cornell in the article on the Chinese congregations.
- Are there parallels to be drawn with work in cultures of the UK which are not based on a different language group? If there are, what are they?

Henry Venn, General Secretary of the Church Missionary Society in the mid nineteenth century, proposed that churches planted by the society should be 'Self-governing, Self-supporting and Self-propagating'.
- Could (or should) this be applied in the UK today and if so how?

Further Reading

Newbigin, L, *The Gospel in a Pluralist Society*, SPCK, London, 1989

Allen, Roland, *Missionary Methods – St Paul's or Ours?*, Eerdemans, Grand Rapids, 1962 (originally published 1927)

Fresh Expressions

Why do we need fresh expressions?

. . . .

We live in an ever-changing world. Cultures and communities continue to change and at an increasing pace. Contemporary British society is characterised by diversity and choice. Lifestyles and leisure pursuits vary, TV and radio channels multiply, internet sites and broadcasting produce virtual communities, work and family patterns change. Despite all these changes there is still a need for community and face-to-face encounter. These developments and more mean that the mission field in Britain is changing. Fresh expressions are forms of church for a changing world.

Five major changes in British society particularly affect the life and mission of the Church.

Changing Sundays. Many people, particularly younger people, work on Sundays. For others, Sunday is a day for sport, or essential time to be with family – this is especially true for divorced parents and their children. People need opportunities for worship and fellowship on other days.

Changing relationships. Where we live use to be the prime determinate of our relationships. We knew our neighbours by name and sometimes appeared in their home unannounced. Parents and other close relatives lived near by and it wasn't unusual to marry 'the girl or boy next door'. Nowadays, relationships are often formed through 'networks' at work or places of leisure. People move around the country to study or develop their career. Today it is not unusual to marry 'the boy who was born 300 miles away'. The Church needs to learn how to relate to different networks and a much more mobile population.

Changing culture. In the past British culture was more homogenous. Regional variations have always been apparent and Britain wouldn't be Britain without its class-consciousness. But there was more of a sense of stability and the churches were a central part of that stability, often being seen as part of the core identity of a region or class. Today we find a multiplicity of groups and subcultures, within regions and socio economic groups, as well as between them. The Church is no longer central to these changing patterns of culture. Yet God calls us to share the good news with all cultures and groups.

Changing understanding of Christianity. Survey after survey still suggests that a majority of British people believe in God and claim to be Christian but fewer and fewer show any signs of commitment to Christian faith. The emerging generations are post-Christian generation. About 4% of children go to Sunday School today. When their great grandparents went to Sunday School they would have gone with 55% of their friends. For children and adults alike we need new forms of church for those who need to begin at the very beginning.

Changing from religious to spiritual. Research suggests that the late 1980s was a low point for spirituality in Britain. 'Greed is good', 'There's no such thing as society' – these were the mantras of the time. Throughout the nineties and into the twenty-first century many have observed a growing interest in spirituality. This can be seen everywhere from the church candles on the shelves of Woolworths to the pages of the celebrity magazines busy discussing Madonna's latest spiritual preference. Spirituality is very much in vogue. Religion however is not. Organised religion has had an image problem for many years. Recently this has been compounded by world events and atrocities committed by those claiming to act in the name of one faith or another. We need forms of church for post religious, pro-spiritual seekers. Why do we need fresh expressions? Because we live in an ever changing world. This, of course, is nothing new. Throughout Christian history new forms of church have emerged as times and needs have changed. Around the world new forms of church continue to emerge, relevant to the context in which they live and move and have their being.

Who are fresh expressions for?

. . . .

Those with little or no Christian experience

The Fresh Expressions definition (p.14) highlights the key group of people for whom fresh expressions are urgently needed. The majority of people in Britain who have no contact with the Christian Church or faith beyond the occasional visit for a baptism, wedding or funeral. When *Mission-shaped Church*[23] was published in 2004 the research behind the report indicated that this was 60% of the population, a proportion that is increasing all of the time as fewer and fewer children and young people have any awareness of Christianity beyond their RE lessons at school.

We live in a new missionary age. If we are to share the good news of the gospel then we need fresh, culturally relevant ways of being church alongside the established churches (that can still connect very well with millions of people) as part of what Archbishop Rowan Williams has called, a 'mixed economy' church.

In recent years, courses such as *Alpha* have been very fruitful in helping people explore the Christian faith and come to a point of commitment. Happily, many of these people have gone on to grow in their faith and discipleship through the life of an established church. Many others, however, have struggled to find a church that reflects the *Alpha* experience, with its meals, relaxed settings and small group discussions. Alpha and other similar courses can be womb like experiences. There is safety and warmth but when the new born emerges from the course the church waiting to greet them may not be best able to help the young Christian grow.

As well as the 60% of the population with little or no connection with the Christian faith there are two other groups of people for whom fresh expressions are particularly important.

The 'de-churched'

Alan Jamieson, a minister from New Zealand, researched why people leave their churches and their journeys of faith outside the Church. He published his findings in *A Churchless Faith*.[24] Amongst the reasons for people leaving were two that cry out for fresh expressions:

[23] *Mission-shaped Church:* Church House Publishing:2004

[24] Alan Jamieson: *A Churchless Faith:* SPCK: 2002

1. People leave when the culture of their church is alien to that of the rest of their lives. Often this will be most evident in the style of worship and particularly in the music. It can also be manifest in children's activities, fellowship groups and even social gatherings. Most classrooms and homes have computers and DVDs – how many Sunday School groups have these?

2. People move on to a churchless faith when they feel their faith has outgrown their church. Professor James Fowler (referred to by Alan Jamieson) identifies seven stages of faith that Christians can go through during a lifetime. If people are growing through the stages but their church is closed to the changes taking place in their lives, they may well leave. We need to be open enough to consider if this is God's will for them.

Whilst fresh expressions are essentially a missionary enterprise, some are needed and will come into being for those who are on the fringes of established churches. They need fresh expressions both for their own spiritual growth and to share their faith with their non Christian friends with whom they share a common culture.

If we are to engage with those presently beyond the reach of the church we need those who can be witnesses to them. Many of these witnesses will be amongst the de-churched.

Communities where the chapel has closed

'I've just bought a Methodist church', said a businessman friend, the day before these words were written. Across the country the rate of chapel closures is increasing. For those involved, the closure of a chapel can be a time of real grief and loss as they mourn for a place that has been very precious to them for a long time. Special, not least because they have had many profound experiences of the love of God there.

The Christian message is based on a story of death and resurrection. Many fresh expressions live out this story. They begin where something dies, a society, a chapel, a way of doing something that has stayed the same for many years before slowly dwindling away. There is a period of mourning before the light of resurrection appears bringing new light and new vision. People discover what it means to be church without a chapel. This is particularly important in small rural communities.

One man in such a community was saddened when his local, much loved chapel closed. The congregation moved to local community centre for worship. A few months later he was on the phone to a friend and said, 'You know I haven't enjoyed church as much for ages. For years I sat in the chapel wondering which tile would fall off the roof next. Now I can sit back, relax and really enjoy worship.'

A fresh expression had brought new life.

What a fresh expression is not...

· · · · · · · · · · · · · · · · · · · ·

Fresh expressions are not ways to get people to church. This is a popular misconception. It is revealed by the often asked question; 'When are they going to come to church?' meaning, 'When are they going to become like us and join in with what we do?' Church activities intended to be a stepping stone for people to come to what we already do are not fresh expressions of church. They may be 'fresh expressions of church life' and as such, good things for the church to start. Fresh expressions of church must have the potential to become church, in its fullness, and with all its responsibilities, in their own right.

Fresh expressions are not merely entertainment. Nothing could be further from the truth. Fresh expressions are based on the same demands for disciples to follow Jesus as all forms of church. They need to be judged by the same yardsticks ad other expressions of church. Do they evangelise, serve, learn and care, worship? When we measure fresh expressions against such yardsticks we must be aware of the need to apply the same to the expressions of church which we already have. Having said that fresh expressions are not merely entertainment, there is nothing wrong with any way of being church being entertaining and attractive.

Fresh expressions are not a re-branding of what we already do. God is always renewing the Church, and we must rejoice in that. Since 2004 there has been a proliferation of fresh and refreshed activity within the life of the Church which is most welcome. But we need to be careful of using language loosely. It is important to note the 'of church' in the definition of a fresh expression. We need fresh expressions that are or have the potential to be fully church for those involved.

Fresh expressions are not superior to other expressions of church.

They are alternative, but all forms of church that express the mission of God in their context and are meeting God's purposes are valuable to God. We must be careful not to fall into one of the traps of a consumerist culture, that of the 'superiority of the new'. Nor must we jump on the latest bandwagon just because it is the latest.

Fresh expressions are not a quick fix.

The development of a fresh expression of church needs long term commitment and resourcing. It cannot be the cure for an already dead church. It may hasten the end of such a church, which has fulfilled its purpose. There are situations where the last gift of a dying church is to make space for something new. Out of its ashes of a church that has died may rise something which is a fresh expression. You cannot have resurrection without death.

Fresh expressions are not new denominations in the making.

Because they are different and introduce new diversity in a denomination there can be tensions, but there is no need for schism. Martin Wellings, in his article, tells of the development of the Central Halls at the end of the nineteenth century. They were significant but did not lead to schism. Neither, in another context, did the development of the Franciscan order in the Roman Catholic Church. Both fresh expression and the denomination and local traditional churches hold responsibility for keeping unity. There is however a need for generosity and flexible attitudes. Sometimes, in the development of a fresh expression, God asks us to step out of the boat of our denominational ways of doing things and to walk on the waters of the future; to step out of the safety of what was good in God's sight yesterday into the uncertainty of tomorrow.

A language of 'blessing' has been adopted by Fresh Expressions to describe an attitude of existing churches and denominational structures to the development of fresh expressions of church. We believe fresh expressions to be a work of the Holy Spirit. We cannot speak of giving permission to the Holy Spirit! Rather God calls those who have been blessed to bless others. Abraham was called so that 'the nations might be blessed' [Genesis 18:18]. The call of God to those who have been blessed with resources is to bless others with no expectation of return, 'to give and not to count the cost'.

If we are to hope that fresh expressions of church will want to be in connexion, it will not be because they are held by Standing Orders but by bonds of relationship and love. Connexion is not about rules but is about relationships.

47

The Wesley Play House

case study

Caroline Holt

In 2005 the 19 members of Howden Clough Methodist Church in Yorkshire were faced with the decline of a mostly elderly congregation and real questions about the future. Closure was an option with possible amalgamation with another church. Instead, they chose radical reformation.

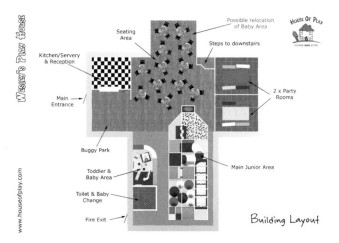

Building Layout

Wesley's Play House

www.houseofplay.com

After many meetings and much prayer they decided to rethink how they served their local community. By June 2007 their building will have re-opened as 'The Wesley Play House'. The building will provide an indoor play area for children and a café for watching parents which will double as a café style worship area.

The creation of 'The Wesley Playhouse' comes from the vision of six of the congregation praying for where the church at Howden Clough could make a difference in the community.
The history of the church has revolved around young people and has seen a Sunday school of over 300 in its heyday. As numbers dwindled we looked at various ways the church could again be at the heart of the community. It was with this in mind that Caroline Holt suggested a very different way forward - that of renovating the main part of the church into a children's play area. After looking at local trends, in her role as a teacher, she saw the potential of offering a service that many families use regularly. After visiting many commercially run playhouses, Caroline, along with three other members, sat down and worked out what the church could offer that people would want. From this the vision for The Wesley Playhouse evolved; the aim is to provide a Fair Trade café with Christian literature available for those using the facility. The Local Authority Early Years Service is so impressed with the concept and plans that they want to make the centre a training base when the playhouse opens.

Views of the Play Areas
from the seating area

www.houseofplay.com

The hope is that, as people come with their children, events will be planned to invite them too. The first planned is 'Playhouse Praise' - month after the playhouse is opened. This will offer all-age worship in the café area of the playhouse, giving alternative ways of worshipping for those not familiar with church, followed by fellowship and food.

From this event it is hoped to offer courses for those interested in finding out more about Christianity, possibly running an Alpha Course, Essence or something similar.

We have engaged local Christians to provide cakes and plan to have a team of volunteers who will help staff the café and share their faith in a very practical way. Our main aim is to live out the Christian faith in a way that challenges people and gives them opportunities to explore their own faith or lack of one. We can only hope and pray God will bless this bold step of faith from a church that in all probability would not be in existence in five years if we continued as we have always done and expect people to just turn up on Sunday and join the church. So watch this space and pray with us that this will be a success story that goes from strength to strength.

Questions

Changing your building will not make you a 'fresh expression'.

- **What is it about the changes being made at Howden Clough that indicate that it is a fresh expression?**
- **When is a fresh expression not a fresh expression?**
- **For those who are at the edges of our existing churches should we try to integrate them into what we have or bless and support them in the development of something more in keeping with their culture?**

Spirituality and Discipleship

Inherited or traditional forms of church tend to concentrate on worship events. Traditional 'church plants' were born when the first service for public worship happened. Denominations count 'bums on seats on Sundays' to determine success. This may have been appropriate in a nation where Christian faith was assumed but that is no longer the case in the UK. In our post-Christian society churches need to reassess their priorities and, we believe, put more emphasis on discipleship and spirituality.

A spirituality of fresh expressions

. . . .

Colin Brown CA [26]

The spirituality of many fresh expressions reflects the rich diversity of the times in which we find ourselves ministering. Although the Church is called, and the Spirit equips it, to reflect the uniqueness of God and the gospel, the present cultural emphasis upon personal choice as opposed to a common meta-narrative[25] is reflected in the plethora of spiritualities within the many examples developing in this country. This is no surprise when we consider the starting point of listening well to both God and context. For each leadership team will be discerning an appropriate missional approach through the lens of their own inherited spirituality, as well as responding to the needs of the people and context.

[25] A 'meta-narrative' (master or grand narrative) is an undergirding story which underlies belief systems of life stances. For example, the meta-narrative of humanity's fall and redemption has been the meta narrative for Western society for more than 1000 years but is no longer the meta-narrative for our society.

[26] Colin is a Church Army officer seconded to the Fresh Expressions Core Team.

The challenge however is to hold lightly to what we bring with us, even to let it die. This is the common thread of fresh expressions spirituality. Many practitioners are being called to step into unknown territory… daily. It has been described as an 'As we go' spirituality. Or even an 'Oh heck!… I have no idea where to go next with this… but I believe God does'. There's a common call, to trust in the God who is always ahead of where we are. To trust that he will lead and reveal the way, step by step and moment by moment. Often leaders say that they feel uneasy when they are trying to make things happen, but spiritually 'at ease' when they have the courage under God to let go… and let God be God, *to* them, and *through* them. Letting go is never easy, especially within a culture of self-interest and protection. Perhaps it is no surprise that the Spirit is calling and equipping a mission-shaped Church to follow in the way of Christ. A spirituality of faith and trust, death and resurrection.

Fresh expressions are just that, fresh. Any description of spirituality in fresh expressions can be no more than a snapshot at a particular time and from a particular place. God's people, in whatever form of church they are found, are a covenant people, in a living relationship with God. In this ever-changing relationship God's people are ever learning new things about God and creation. It is in this context that Colin Brown's description is neither definitive nor prescriptive.

52

Discipleship in fresh expressions

. . . .

Fresh expressions of church are not ends in themselves. It is not the number of specific projects that will determine the fruitfulness of the Conference priority and ecumenical initiative. Rather it is the extent of loving service, the quality of community and the depth of discipleship that emerges which will be the true indicators of fruitfulness. If fresh expressions are to be a lasting and natural part of the life of a mixed economy church then they need to be communities of good soil in which the seeds of the gospel can grow to maturity. Without good discipleship there is a real risk that fresh expressions can be communities of shallow soil in which seeds spring up quickly and enthusiastically but then whither equally rapidly when the novelty of the new fades away.

'When dealing with discipleship, and the related capacity to generate authentic followers of Jesus, we are dealing with that single most crucial factor that will in the end determine the quality of the whole – if we fail at this point then we must fail in all the others.'

Alan Hirsch[27]

Questions of discipleship are key in both fresh and established expressions of church. The foundational importance of discipleship has been strongly reaffirmed within the Methodist Church in recent years. The success of *Time to Talk of God*[28] and the Presidential themes of Graham Carter and (Youth President) Rob Redpath have all served to highlight the call to discipleship which is common to all Christians.

[27] Hirsch, Alan *The Forgotten Ways* Brazos 2006

[28] *Time to Talk of God* The Methodist Church 2005

Discipleship groups should develop as they will, inside or outside of the current structures of the Church. As at the beginning, fresh expressions of church must start with discipleship and we have to accept that the Church as we presently know it may not be able to contain them.

Graham Carter, President of Conference 2006/7

If churches, fresh or established, are to be 'good soil communities' then three things need to be present:

- clear discipleship **values**,

- appropriate and supportive **relationships**,

- relevant and engaging ways of **learning**.

Values are key in shaping our practices and behaviour. When forming fresh expressions it is vital that careful attention is paid to the foundational values of the new community. This is particularly true in the area of discipleship. Within the fresh expressions movement there is a growing appreciation of the need for *whole life* discipleship, whole life in the sense of lifelong - recognising that there are issues of discipleship in childhood, youth and all stages of adulthood. Also whole life in the sense of every part of life, the sacred and the secular, at work, home, in the community and even in church. In this new missional age there is an urgent need for discipleship formation through which we help each other to live holistic, missional Christian lives wherever God calls us to be. *Time to Talk of God* contains an excellent overview of discipleship values.

Within most fresh expressions there is a strong emphasis on relationships and community. There is a lot of eating, laughing, learning and praying *together*. The breaking of bread, sharing of lives and supporting of one another in mission are key values for many newly forming churches.

The Methodist Class system is often cited as an excellent relational model for the formation of discipleship. Sadly, this is more of a memory than a present reality in much of contemporary British Methodism. However, the growth in housegroups, discipleship courses (such as *Disciple* and *Emmaus*), the Cell Church movement and Covenant Discipleship have all re-emphasized the key role of the small group in nurturing discipleship. Small groups are not the only helpful discipling relationship model. Others include discipleship companions (Luke 24:13-35) and mentors/apprentices (for an example Paul and Timothy, Acts 16-20 and 1 and 2 Timothy).

In an age when café church is cool it is important that new ways of being church do not just serve cappuccino froth to nurture disciples. Good learning practices are crucial for all ages. In the present post-modern, post-Christian age we can assume very little prior knowledge or understanding of Christian discipleship. In fresh expressions in particular we need learning approaches that:

- start where people are,
- assume very little in terms of prior understanding,
- allow for questioning and exploration,
- are culturally relevant and engaging,
- related to the lives people lead,
- emphasise both the adventure and the cost of true discipleship.

Within the Connexion and the Fresh Expressions team much is being done to encourage the formation of good discipleship relationships, resources and practices. Connexional officers and Fresh Expressions team members are part of a 'Round Table' consultation group that draws together leading discipleship resource providers and fresh expressions practitioners.

Bible Study

Read the parable of the sower (or soils) Matthew 13:1-13 and 13:18-23.

- What do you need for there to be good soil in which disciples can grow to maturity?
- What shortcomings in values, relationships or learning approaches might result in a church community (fresh or established) becoming shallow soil?

Read Acts 2:42-46

- In Luke's pen portrait of the early Church what were the key features of a fruitful church?

Activity

- Write a discipleship charter for your church, outlining the values, relationships and learning approaches you see as key to forming whole life, missionary disciples. **Or**
- Make a model of a discipleship garden and plant some seeds in it. As you make and tend the garden reflect on the parable of the sower. What makes the soil good, or otherwise? Apart from the soil, what else do the seeds need to grow?

Safe Space

Andrew Roberts

Safe Space is an emerging missional community based in Telford. The community describes itself as a group of 'spiritual seekers, God reachers and Christ followers'. The focus of Safe Space is to engage with people in thier 20's and 30's, in particular those for whom traditional church has no resonance, but no door is closed. The community is on a new spiritual journey beyond the traditional structures and cultures of the church.

Mark Berry leads the community and describes their core discipleship values as:

- incarnational living,
- mentoring/Soul Friends,
- shared journey – walking with people, following Christ,
- rhythm of prayer, Scripture and community,
- reflective theology, spirituality and praxis,
- risky living,
- global/local involvement and responsibility.

Disciples are nurtured through relationships, by demonstration/incarnation, living and encouraging reflection in terms of Scripture, story and experience. Members of the community encourage one another to find God in the ordinary and everyday, in action and in creation

Sacred Space places a great deal of emphasis on daily rhythm and liturgy, a weekly meal and meditation. The community breaks bread before every meal. All of these help to build mutual accountability and encouragement. The journey of discipleship is furthered by pilgrimages that are undertaken in pairs and as a community.

Worship and
the Sacraments

'If 'church' is what happens when people encounter the risen Jesus and commit themselves to sustaining and deepening that encounter in their encounter with each other, there is plenty of theological room for diversity of rhythm and style, so long as we have ways of identifying the same living Christ at the heart of every expression of Christian life in common.'

Archbishop Rowan Williams

Anglican Church in Galle, Sri Lanka, just north of the equator.

If fresh expressions are church they will express themselves in worship of God. As part of this they will share in the sacraments of Baptism and Holy Communion.

Our changing culture is challenging the Church. The development of fresh expressions is part of the Church's response. The Church is responding in all areas of our life, including worship. There are no templates for worship in fresh expressions of church.

Fresh expressions are expressions of church in communities where people are not already members of a church. In the days of the British Empire churches were planted abroad that looked little different to those in Britain, in liturgy, organisation and buildings. We learned from our mistakes – eventually – that church needs to be expressed in the culture of the people who make up that church – without giving up the aspects of the gospel that challenge any and every culture to become holy.

Fresh expressions of church in the cultures of twenty first century Britain also need to be expressed in the culture of the people concerned.

Roland Allen, a missiologist who was a missionary in China at the time of the Boxer rebellion/liberation struggle, wrote an analysis of missionary methods of his time. His basic argument is that St Paul, in planting churches, never stayed more than three years. By that time he had established:

- leadership,

and given the church

- the Scriptures,
- a means of interpreting the Scriptures (creeds),
- the sacraments of Holy Communion and Baptism.

Paul then trusted the new church and God. We know from the epistles that this was not always an easy way of working! As the churches developed in their context problems arose. Rather than just trying to avoid problems and even failure, which is impossible anyway, we need to be prepared to learn from them.

The fresh expressions of church that became the Salvation Army and the Society of Friends (Quakers) challenge our views of church. They are made up of Christians, they meet for worship, they learn and care, they serve and they do evangelism. They fit *Our Calling* and

as such they express 'church', but they do not share the sacraments of Baptism and Holy Communion. Does this make them less 'church' than those who do?

Working from Roland Allen's missionary principles, the way the sacraments are expressed in a fresh expression may be somewhat different to the way they are expressed in a traditional church. The same applies to worship.

The Methodist formula for worship, taught to all local preachers and worship leaders involved various elements of hymns and songs, prayers, Bible readings and a sermon or talk(s). In a fresh expression any of these might be present but in different ways.

Legacy XS is a church established in a skateboard culture. Worship in that culture can include skateboard and BMX bike 'tricks'. People from this church observe that this is similar to the use of dance in more traditional forms of church. They are the gift to God of a person giving of their talents in worship.

Xpresso 6:15 in Lincoln is a café style worship event in which refreshments are served throughout and in which contemporary film plays a key part. The format of the event is also different from the traditional in that part of it is 'multiple choice', a time when people can choose from a range of different expressions of spirituality; a quiet zone, a discussion group, a place for intercessory prayer, a place for shared prayer, a tactile zone where worship can be expressed using the sense of touch…. and more.

The Goth Eucharist, the Anglican church of St Edward, King and Martyr in Cambridge, is very traditional in many ways. Rooted in Catholic spirituality, expressing something very old indeed - the mass, but expressed in a fresh way to be relevant to a marginalised community. http://www.thegotheucharist.org.uk/

'Christians are challenged to live and witness to their faith in all parts of their lives and in every place. I am impressed that those of the Goth Eucharist are working out this challenge; going where only few of the Church venture and seeking an expression of the Christian gospel in terms that are distinct and new.'

Right Revd Robert Ladds,
Bishop of Whitby

As fresh expressions develop we need to find ways of making space for them to develop their worship and sacramental life in diverse ways that may challenge us to review how we express ours.

Questions

Some Christians (for example those from the Society of Friends [Quakers] and The Salvation Army) say that every meal shared together by Christians is sacramental.
- **What do you think?**

- **How would you react to a teenager using a skateboard in the worship you share in?**

Think carefully through the worship of your church over the past year.
- **Are there any ways of worship you use that have come from 'foreign' cultures?**
- **Are there parts of your worship that would be 'foreign' to Christians of other traditions?**
- **Are there aspects of your worship that might be 'foreign' to your friends and neighbours who are not part of a church?**

(A clue – if you would have to explain something you do to a visitor then it is 'foreign' to them)

In South India, some Christians celebrate Jesus' death and resurrection using a coconut instead of bread and wine. The coconut is part of a local staple diet. The coconut is broken open and the liquid and flesh shared in a similar way to us breaking bread and sharing wine.
- **Is this Holy Communion?**

A mixed economy church

'I've talked quite a bit about the church of the future as a mixed economy, meaning by this that there's no one kind of church life that captures everything, that does every kind of job.

We need both a traditional parish doing its work really well and some quite new kinds of venture, some new kinds of initiative, that's what I mean by a mixed economy and I think that's where the health of the church of the future is going to lie.'

Archbishop Rowan Williams

Archbishop Rowan Williams in a series of talks broadcast by the BBC coined the term 'mixed economy'.

Does the need for and emergence of fresh expressions spell the end of church as we know it? By no means!

Traditional church is still helpful and meaningful for up to 40% of the population – a lot of people. We need to continue to resource, develop and grow established churches through:

- being a welcoming and open community,
- offering ways for all ages to learn about faith,
- worship and preaching that have depth and relevance,
- inviting people into life-changing discipleship and service.

These values are at the heart of fresh expressions too.

Established churches and fresh expressions. Both are needed if we are to serve the present age and make disciples of Jesus in our contemporary cultures.

Basic Methodist structures do not need to change to develop such a mixed economy. The fundamental unit for the oversight of mission in Methodism is the circuit. Within any circuit a wide variety of forms of church are possible. The circuit is responsible for 'neighbourhoods' but Home Mission guidelines for House Congregations, adopted by Conference in 1987, note that neighbourhoods may not only be based on geography but can also be based on networks or relationships.

There are a number of necessary changes of mindset needed to encourage fresh expressions:

- From 'possible' to 'normal' and 'necessary'. This must be recognized in changes in the way presbyters, deacons, local preachers and other officers are selected and trained. In this we may do well to learn from the examples from the world church given above.
- We need to be able to bless without expecting a return. To give and not to count the cost. To labour and not to seek for any reward save that of knowing we do God's will. Fresh expressions are not about building a Methodist kingdom, or one of any denomination.

A mixed economy church then is one where the church has a strategy for accepting and promoting cultural diversity and is willing to treasure that diversity. In particular in the present context it is one that seeks to develop the best of what we at present have, whilst making room and finding resources for the development of the new and different.

Pause for thought

The Greek word μετανοια (metanoia), literally means 'a change of mind'. It can mean repentance, remorse, or conversion.

We tend to think of conversion as something that happens to individual people at a particular time.

Does the church need to be converted?

Is sin institutional as well as personal?

How might an institution show it is being converted?

Nettleham Methodist Church

Pete Pillinger/
Mark Lawrence

As God's Spirit prompts the initiation of completely new Christian communities, so the Spirit also renews Christian communities that are prepared to change. Nettleham Methodist Church, in a village north of Lincoln, has planted fresh expressions of church for more than 20 years and has been in transition to Cell Church for the last ten years…

In Nettleham, a traditional church had grown from a small village congregation of less than 20 to a church of 120 through the development of multiple, parallel, congregations. By the early 1990's the church had three Sunday morning congregations reaching three groups of people through worship in different styles. One congregation ended after a group of its leaders left the Methodist Church in 1994. Of the remaining two congregations one is traditional and one 'contemporary'.

With any church based on congregations (large groups of people in this case between 70 and 100) there is a danger that people will not be noticed when they are not there. There were holes in the local pastoral 'net' and action was needed.

The church council decided to encourage exploration of ways of restoring the Methodist Class system by exploring Cell Church values and principles.

The idea of Cell Church is that people are part of a small group as well as a congregation. The Cell (which parallels the traditional Methodist Class) is understood to be 'church' just as the congregation is – both are expressions of church, both are valuable.

Eight years later 75% of those who attend Sunday worship are also part of a small Christian community or 'Cell'. In addition, 75% of those involved in Cells are also involved in Sunday worship. New Cells are born through a process that involves the Cells being outward looking and the use of the Alpha Course.

About 12% of the population of Nettleham is at present actively involved in the life of a Christian community. This includes the local Anglican church, a 'new' church and others who are involved in churches outside the village. The Methodist and Anglican churches, along with the 'new' church, are now working together to raise this proportion to 20% by 2012.

For more information on Cell Church see the Resources section at the end of this book.

Fresh expressions should be enabled to be part of the whole Body of Christ, but that does not mean making them fit traditional structures. We can't expect all Christ's disciples to become members of the Methodist Church, or any other church for that matter. The Holy Spirit is not bound by earthly structures.

Graham Carter, President of Conference 2006/7

Holding the mixed economy together

. . . .

Methodism is rightly proud of being a connexional church. If we are to become more diverse in our expressions of church what is to hold us together?

Our faith speaks of a triune God, a God who is three in one. In the Trinity, diversity and unity are held together in a creative relationship. It is this triune God whose mission we share in.

The Nicene Creed describes a Church that is 'one holy, catholic and apostolic'. Methodists, in affirming this formula for understanding the nature of the Church, are connected with most other denominations. Fresh expressions of church, like any other form of church, can be tested against this description.

Within a Methodist context we speak of being in 'Connexion', a concept that speaks of the unity of the Church. We recognise that we need to hold relationship with churches throughout the world. We recognise that there is a unity underlying the diversity of the world Church that is based on our common faith in Jesus Christ.

We believe we are fully part of this 'catholic' or universal Church. We share a common call to 'spread scriptural holiness through the proclamation of the evangelical faith'[29] and we 'rejoice in the inheritance of the apostolic faith'.[30] One of the hallmarks, then, of Methodism is a belief in the unity of the Church that is expressed through 'Connexion'. This will be true of fresh expressions – and of all other expressions of church. The telling of the stories which you read here are not an encouragement to do things outside that 'Connexion'. Rather we believe that fresh expressions of church need the support and encouragement that can be received only in 'Connexion' with other churches.

The Methodist involvement in the Fresh Expressions initiative springs from the *Our Calling* process. In this process, a common, simple understanding of what it means to be Church has been expounded. We are called to Service, Evangelism, Learning and Caring and Worship.[31] Each of these four quadrants is necessary for the full expression of

[29] Deed of Union Section 2 Clause 4 Doctrinal standards

[30] Ibid.

[31] The change from the normal order of these in *Our Calling* reflects the way fresh expressions start. More often this is in loving service and ending in worship rather than the other way round.

what it means to be Church. Part of the challenge of fresh expressions of church to the Connexion is to realise that the four quadrants of *Our Calling* should be part of the life of all our churches, not just of fresh expressions of church.

We can encourage the development of a mixed economy church if we are willing to learn lessons from those involved. Connexion is not about fresh expressions conforming to existing ways of being church. Connexion is also a call to the Church to '*adapt its structures as it faces new situations and challenges*'.[32] Many fresh expressions of church arise among people for whom denominational loyalty means little. So we need ask, '*Why should a fresh expression of church wish to be in connexion with us?*'

We also need to encourage fresh expressions of what we already do – renewal of the Church for mission is not by replacing what we already are. It is a both/and process not an either/or.

'The circuit is the primary unit in which local churches express and experience their interconnexion in the body of Christ, for purposes of mission, mutual encouragement and help.' S.O.500

[32] *Called to Love and Praise* 4.7.11

Questions

- How can we hold traditional and fresh expressions of church together and aid them understanding each other?

- In a Church of growing diversity what makes us Methodist?
  (You may want to study this further, not just in the context of fresh expressions of church. Called to Love and Praise is a good resource)

- If fresh expressions of church really are church and not just experimental adjuncts to the traditional church, how do they and traditional church relate?
- How do we convince Methodist people that more resources should go to fresh expressions away from traditional'?
- If resurrection only comes after death – in what ways can we do this in church life? What things might need to die in order to leave room for resurrection? How do you decide?
- Why should a fresh expression of church wish to be in connexion with the Methodist church?

Bible Study

Read:
- Mark 3:16-19
- Acts 2:5-21
- Galatians 3:26-28
- Romans 12:1-10

Investigate each of the disciples and their origins. What held this diverse group together?

What does the Acts 2 story of the nations who heard in their own language, tell us of the way God works?

What do the passages from the epistles tell you of holding together diversity?

Further questions
for a Methodist mixed economy church

It is not our intention here to specify ways in which the structures of the Methodist Church might respond to enable the development of 'fresh ways of being church'. However, we raise the following points for discussion.

- **Local preachers and worship leaders** - How is 'fresh ways of being church' reflected in local preacher and worship leader training (initial and continuing)?

- **Class leaders** - it is the weekly Class meeting that 'has from the beginning proved to be the most effective means of maintaining among Methodists true fellowship in Christian experience.' President Graham Carter's call to discipleship, if taken seriously, will lead us back to our roots as a movement of small Christian communities. It is the observation of fresh expressions that some sort of discipling group structure is foundational to the development of most fresh expressions of church. We note that while:
  - o Class leaders are the first appointment for local churches in Standing Orders (section 63 – Principal Officers);

and:
  - o the guidelines on house congregations approved by Conference in 1987 gave Class leaders responsibility to see that Methodist events happen within our doctrine and discipline;

that:
  - o while the Church has put a large proportion of its resources into training local preachers and ministers it has put very little, if any, resources into the training of Class leaders. With a renewal of interest in discipleship and clear understanding that the nurture of disciples happens best in small groups, this is an urgent need.

- **Workers with children and young people**
  There are ten times as many people working with children and young people as there are ministers. About a quarter of those involved in fresh expressions of church are children. Youth congregations are one of the most popular genres of fresh expressions. We will need to do some serious thinking about the place of workers with children and young people.

A lay led movement

The majority of those who are involved in all types of fresh expression are lay people. Many fresh expressions are lay led. This gives new opportunities for local preachers and worship leaders. If we are to increase the numbers of fresh expressions developed through the Methodist Church we will need more leaders. Cell Church, one of the types of fresh expression mentioned in *Mission-shaped Church*, has been described as not only being a system for development of discipleship in the Church but also a leadership multiplication tool. The development of fresh expressions will need new forms of leadership and rethinking the roles of some of those that already exist.

Questions

- How might the local preachers/worship leaders of your circuit be involved in developing fresh expressions in your circuit?
- How will your church and circuit encourage discipleship groups and the role of class leader?
- In a lay led movement, how do we enable the sacramental life of fresh expressions?
- What is the place of the circuit?
- Angela Tillby, a speaker on the Fresh Expressions Hard Questions tour in spring 2007, spoke of a 'mixed ecology' rather than a 'mixed economy'. Which of these terms speaks most powerfully to you and what differences do you perceive?

Starting

We all know that understanding the theory and the need is one thing; the situation on the ground may well be another.

What would your church or circuit do if someone said 'God has called me to develop a fresh expression of church in ……. our village/town/city.'?
Jesus told a parable of a wedding feast. When the feast was ready, the master sent his servants to fetch the guests. 'I have bought a cow.' 'I have married a new wife.' 'I have other things to do.' It is easy to be so focussed on what we already do that we cannot see beyond its horizon. God, however, constantly challenges us to think outside our limits. This is not easy for most of us – but it is our calling.

There is no fresh expressions equivalent of painting by numbers, no detailed 'off the shelf' plan for your situation. Every fresh expression is different because every situation is different. The Fresh Expressions courses mentioned in the Resources section at the end of this book are designed to give the tools for you to work out what you may need to do where you are.

Use the situations below to explore possibilities. They may spark your thinking about a local situation that you know in more detail.

The circuit:

- Could experiment with models of church attractive to particular groups of people, without jeopardising the essential unity of the Methodist Church,
- Can encourage a variety of expressions of church alongside opportunities for those who attend to meet in united fellowship from time to time,
- Is uniquely positioned to offer a combination of serving geographical communities and communities of interest.

Models for Mission, Trustees for Methodist Church Purposes 2006

Imagine a university city with thousands of students – but with only a handful involved in your church or circuit. Less than one percent of the students have any connection with local churches. In addition to the students, thousands more people aged under 40 from the city and surrounding area are drawn into a vibrant club culture. Binge drinking is rife along with behaviour related to it.

Jenny, a young person of 22, recently back from her own university studies and with an active Christian faith, knocks at the superintendent minister's door. She has an intense feeling of God's call to see an expression of church established which will touch her peers but knows that none of the churches in the circuit can be it, nor do they have the spare resources, or the people to tackle the calling.

- How is such a vision and calling to be tested?
- Can the circuit catch the vision?
- Are they big enough to take the risk of supporting Jenny?
- Will they pray and pay for this new work?
- Will the ministers want to bless the work or are they too busy keeping the show on the road?
- Can space be made in the busy timetable of church 'as is' for the support of church 'that might be'?
- Will the churches and circuit be prepared to release and bless people to join Jenny and form a team to develop her fresh expression?
- Will they expect it to be Methodist?
- If the circuit is prepared to support Jenny's calling will they put their money where their mouth is and vote to put Circuit Advance Fund money into supporting the vision?
- How will the fresh expression be accountable to the circuit (or a church?)
- What happens if there are people who 'block' the vision?
- What if the block is among the circuit staff?
- How can the district enable the development of fresh expressions when the local circuit does not have the energy or inclination?
- If the local churches of her denomination will not back her, will Jenny go somewhere else?
- How can the wider church 'authorise' Jenny's call to a particular pioneering ministry?

Questions

The illustration outlines an initiative to reach younger people.

- Which people in your area are unreached by the church 'as is'? (This might not be just young people.)

- How might you help 'church' to develop among such people?

- In an earlier chapter of this book Martin Wellings explored the development of fresh expressions in our history. Look back at that chapter and ask, 'What lessons can we learn from our history?

- How might the appointment of a deacon put an emphasis on fresh expressions in your circuit?

Keeping flexible

A vision may lead people to develop a fresh expression of church. They may make plans and hope that they will be fulfilled. Often fresh expressions develop in ways beyond the hopes of those involved. The Spirit moves and plans must adapt. Fresh expressions must keep flexible. The illustrative story is of a relatively new fresh expression that has grown faster than its founders expected and become more than the planners had envisioned.

Taste and See

Ashley Cooper

In Kidsgrove, a new Christian community has emerged in the last two years based on the desire of some local Christians to reach their secular peers. This desire led to the establishment of a coffee shop (Taste and See) and Christian community in that 'coffee culture'. Working with the local Methodist circuit the group has sought to explore mission and discipleship in a new context. The numbers of people involved have grown rapidly over the last two years – most of those involved are under 40 years old and about half of the people involved are new Christians. Worship, a relaxed multi-media event, happens in the coffee shop on a Wednesday night. The coffee shop is also used for Alpha, prayer breakfasts and other mission-orientated activities.

The Taste and See coffee shop was set up by a group of people all under 35. The small group was asking 'Why are there no people of our age in any of our churches?' They then asked, 'What can we do to get such people to come to our churches?' but realised that this is the wrong question. They went on to ask, 'How can we see church incarnated in our culture, a 'coffee' culture?' and so Taste and See was born.

The need quickly arose to offer more than was practically possible in the small coffee shop context and through relationships and mission the Christian community associated with Taste and See quickly grew to the point where the café was not big enough. All that was pioneered in the café continued and in addition a new church plant was established in a local pub, The Galley. The pub soon became too small and the new church plant now meets in the local town hall. The new Christian community currently has approx 90 adults and 40 young people under 16 and is still growing........

This has raised questions about how The Galley will relate to the circuit and district.

Ashley Cooper, Evangelism Enabler
Chester and Stoke-on-Trent District

Taste and See is featured on
Expressions – the DVD

'If church councils hold the decision making powers over fresh expressions, by their very nature the fresh expressions are not likely to have people who qualify to be members of the church council. It does not seem right that a 'traditional' church council should have executive authority over a fresh expression. On the other hand a fresh expression needs to be accountable if it genuinely part of the Body of Christ, but there is a difference between accountability and control. The twin dangers I see are that,

- on the one hand, church councils could decide to close down what they perceive as 'experiments' because they are not 'bringing people into church' and
- on the other, fresh expressions could hive off independently and become virtually separate denominations.'

Graham Carter, President of Conference 2006/7

Questions

- How flexible do our denominational structures need to be to encourage fresh expressions of church?
- Does our system of 'stationing' ministers need changing to take account of the need for fresh expressions?
- How can our rules and regulations be made to make room for fresh ways of being church which, almost by definition, will not fit the rules?
- Should all fresh expressions of church come under an existing circuit?

Enabling fresh expressions to mature

What does it mean to be a 'mature church' in a Methodist context?
....

How can we enable recognition from circuits and enable fresh expressions to be mature partners in circuit, including financial contribution? Who pays? The circuit may give part of staff time but the fresh expression pays no assessment. Traditional church needs to own the blessing of fresh expressions.

When fresh expressions of church emerge, we need flexible approaches that allow recognition and accountability at church, circuit, district or connexional level.

To start a fresh expression a church or circuit may need to put significant resources in both money and time over a period of five or more years. Eventually the fresh expression must become a mature part of the Connexion. It must, in its turn, help to finance and resource the wider church. There is no template for this process, nor guidance in Standing Orders. This story raises questions about how a fresh expression can achieve maturity as a church in a circuit – one among equals.

Church4u

Pete Pillinger

Part of Pickering Methodist Church in rural North Yorkshire is a fresh expression called Church4U. It was formed by a group of people who felt called to reach people the church did not normally reach. Most of the people in this group were younger than the average for the church and wanted to share their faith with their contemporaries. They knew, however, that the existing church was not likely to attract such people.

Church4U is based on small Christian communities meeting weekly and a fortnightly celebration gathering of these cells. It seeks to be accessible to non-Christian friends of people who are part of Church4u. It operates in parallel with the more traditional church forms.

Both the traditional and Church4U are presently part of Pickering Methodist Church and accountable to the church council but as Church4U has grown and matured questions are being asked about the future nature of this relationship. Church4u has grown to about 50 people, 30 of whom are also part of the traditional Sunday congregation. Some of the leaders of Church4U who are also part of the traditional congregation also serve as church stewards.

Questions

- How can Church4u become a mature expression of church and how can the church and circuit recognise this?
- Should it continue to be part of a local church or is its future as a new church within the circuit?
- Should oversight move from the church council to the circuit meeting?
- Who makes such decisions and how?

Keeping Fresh

It has been said that a tradition is something we did the same way last week. It is easy to get into a rut and lose freshness, whether we are traditional church or a fresh expression. This story tells of an older fresh expression's journey to keep fresh.

How can we keep fresh? What does it take to avoid a 'tendency to rot' – a tendency to keep doing what we did last year without thinking why we still do it or whether it is God's will to do it. 14 years ago a new church was planted in Stoke-on-Trent but being new did not mean they were immune from the challenge to keep fresh.

The Potter's House

Pastor Phil Barber

The church, originally called Birches Head Christian Fellowship, was founded in 1992 by 25 adults and children from Swan Bank Methodist Church, Burslem, and found its first home in the hall of Birches Head High School where we continued to meet for the first 12 years. Our vision was to form a family church serving the needs primarily of the Birches Head estate. Over the years this vision has widened and many people from across the city have joined us so that we have become a truly city wide church.

In November 2005 we succeeded in purchasing the school building where we were meeting to create a community church and enterprise centre called The Bridge Centre. Despite seeing steady growth we felt that the church, as it was, did not attract people from our local community, most of whom were 'unchurched'. We asked ourselves questions such as:

- How relevant and accessible was our worship?
- Why was it that unchurched people did not go to worship?
- How could we communicate the gospel in a more creative and dynamic way?

So in July 2006 we decided to change the name of the church to The Potter's House, to more accurately reflect its mission as a city centre church and to symbolise its reinvention as a church ministering in the 21st century.

One of our biggest challenges was to change the mindset of our people to accept church as being not for us but for the broken, lost and hurting people outside our walls. Our comfort zone was about to be removed so how could we prepare them for that?

As we began to make changes to the style of worship some people felt insecure as familiar things (such as the communion table) began to disappear. A lot of pastoral support was offered but inevitably a few people chose to look for another church. This was quite a painful experience but we pressed ahead with determination to see the process through.

The leadership team had many difficult, frank and challenging discussions because, at times, people felt offended, hurt and confused but we continued to keep praying, forgiving and supporting each other. The pastor had his work cut out!

We introduced things slowly and carefully and tried to explain all the changes as they happened, step by step. We encouraged people to join small groups that helped them to feel they mattered and were supported by those in their group.

Worship was a battlefield. It was no longer enough just to sing and play in worship bands; training was needed to improve skills and become more professional, because that is what unchurched people expect and experience at gigs or concerts. We instituted a system of auditions and a school of worship, and standards are continuing to rise. We decided to change the style of worship and for a while some people missed the old songs. Most have appreciated the new multi media items and we are continuing to learn about how to communicate in visual ways.

Looking outwards, the church was too insular. New people needed to feel they belonged and building relationships was vital. But making these relationships with new, often hurting people, was hard. We created new activities such as welcome meetings and open houses to bring people together. We provided training for the pastoral team and we developed Family Support Services, an action group set up by Christians to offer professional help to hurting people in areas of need such as pregnancy crisis, post abortion, domestic violence, bereavement, debt, and depression.

Fresh ways of being church in a Methodist context

Synod has agreed that the district can sponsor/look after certain fresh expressions, that would be difficult to regulate from a circuit base, using the district evangelism enabler as a link - but this could take up more of his time than is manageable and it puts me (as district chair) in the position of a 'superintendent' of a virtual district circuit of fresh expressions - personally stretching and needing moderatorial skills as it contrasts with standard circuit conditions.'

John D Walker

This comment was made in the context of a desire in the district policy group and synod to link experiments with circuits wherever possible. The district is not setting out to create such a fresh expressions circuit. It is simply looking after projects until they can find a more permanent resting place. The district plans to appoint a small liaison group to link the district with projects and support them – not just leave it indefinitely to the district evangelism enabler alone.

The church is aiming to be relevant, relational and resourcing and is on a journey to discover more about reaching the unchurched in this 21st century. Each person in the church has had to go on their own personal journey which at times has been fun and exciting and at others challenging and exhausting.
In the summer of 2006 we had two choices:

o stay as we were (Birches Head Christian Fellowship) comfortable, cliquey, experiencing transfer growth, maintaining what we had got but gradually dying (growing old together) over a period of time or
o going in a new and radical direction (The Potter's House) breaking down the church walls to enable those in need of a relationship with Jesus to find him and trying to build for the future.

By January 2007 the work on The Bridge Centre was 80% complete and the church has begun to flourish in its new home.

The church has grown steadily throughout its existence to around 400 regular worshippers with a total community roll of more than 500.

Questions

- What lessons can you draw out from the story of The Potter's House?
- What in your church needs to be reassessed?
- When might a fresh expression cease to be 'fresh'?
- What makes it difficult for change to be implemente

Reaching the generations

FE's and young people and the not so young ....

Much of what is happening is rapidly changing. This is particularly true with fresh expressions of church working with younger people. Fresh Expressions strongly advocates processes of learning from experience. We therefore, in this section, are giving most of the space to examples. There are three examples, two are youth based – the other is not! It would be wrong to give the impression that fresh expressions are expressions of church for those under 40. However, it should be recognised that the average age of the Methodist Church is well over that of the general population.

Questions

Read and discuss the three following stories of fresh expressions.
As you read, keep a notepad with you and note ideas that you might be able to use in your church or circuit.
Also, note things that will not work in your situation – and say why.

Revolution -

Learning about the Jesus Revolution

In 2003, Youth for Christ launched Street Space, an initiative intended to reach out to young people living in Inverness. This YFC project began with one youth worker and has developed into a team of four youth workers focusing on one school in the city. The team opened a café style drop-in centre within the school and a number of after school clubs, whilst leading assemblies and taking a role in mentoring young adults. From the start their five-year plan involved developing a fresh expression of church to bridge the gap between youth culture and the practices of the Christian community.

Revolution became a place where young people who wanted to find out more about faith could explore Christian worship. Unlike traditional services Revolution does not involve chorus or hymn singing but a combination of DJ worship, meditative prayer, and Bible study. Often the young people experienced God speaking to them through prophecies and visions. Dave Saunders, the leader of Revolution, shared some experiences with me. In one story he recalls a girl who saw a vision of her enemies and felt God prompting her to pray for them. On another occasion a young lad came to him after school

and speechless and in tears he wrote on a scrap of paper that God had spoken to him for the first time in his life, at Revolution.

Recently, the YFC team have asked four young people to lead a mission in their local community. Dave knew that only two of the young people were Christians and was surprised when the other two young leaders asked him how they could give their lives to God. In a week's time these four young adults will lead their peers in an effort to clean up their local park and paint an old lady's house. Whilst the young people are learning to serve God and their neighbours they are also involved in relational evangelism; inviting their peers along to Revolution and sharing their personal testimonies openly with one another and the team.

Since starting Revolution with 15 young people that number has grown to 25. However, many have moved house, started university, or changed schools. Still, others have grown up through Street Space and Revolution, becoming peer group leaders and evangelists in their own right. They are the first fruits of a new generation of Christians with an age-old message of hope and transformation for the world.

The Vine

Andrew Roberts

In Berkswich, in the Stafford Circuit, on the third Sunday of the month (8 – 9.30pm) a fresh expression for young people called The Vine meets. As with many other fresh expressions, food is a key part of The Vine – everything from chips to cheese being served. There is also a strong emphasis on participation as the young people shape the life of The Vine, finding through it a God who is part of their lives. It is both missional and fun. The Vine's mission statement says that the aim is 'To provide a group of young people from varied faith backgrounds, with a safe and comfortable place to engage with God and Christianity'.

The comfortable space is created by using drapes, soft lighting, giant cushions and other comfy seating to create a room that is part lounge, part nightclub. Community is built through eating and playing together. Faith is shared and explored using a variety of creative media including music and DVD clips, discussion groups, and interactive biblical reflections. Evenings conclude with an informal time of worship led by the young people.

Dave Robson leader of the fresh expression says, 'The Vine is never the same twice. We seek to explore the views and topics we face in life, and create a space where young people can encounter God personally'.

When The Vine meets the hall is full of young people from both church a non church backgrounds. The quality of the fresh expression is such that Christian young people can invite their non Christian friends with confidence.

Fresh ways of being church in a Methodist context

Not just for younger people

Not all fresh expressions are for younger people. We have chosen to give a number of stories based on fresh expressions that are reaching younger people because the Methodist Church is losing younger people at twice the rate we are losing older people. But there are many people of all ages who are open to fresh expressions of church.

The Good Shepherd:

Shrewsbury - A 'virtual' chapel

'The harvest field is plentiful, but the workers are few. Ask the Lord of the harvest, therefore, to send out workers into his harvest field.'

Luke 10:2

If you thought fresh expressions were just about teenagers, data projectors and the music of Matt Redman, think again! In rural Shropshire a fresh expression is growing for the elderly, infirm and housebound. Dubbed a 'virtual' chapel by the Shrewsbury Circuit, the Good Shepherd congregation is congregating in a new way.

In July 2006 Trish Calvert (an Anglican lay person) was commissioned by the circuit to bring the church to the people. This Trish does through spiritual care with regular pastoral visits to the members' homes for fellowship, worship and Holy Communion (for which Trish has been given a dispensation to administer).

Increasingly, members are inviting their friends and neighbours to share in the life of the virtual chapel, so the Good Shepherd is very much a mission-shaped church. Good Shepherd members stay connected to the wider church through Trish's ministry and the sharing of recorded services, DVDs and newsletters.

Speaking about this exciting new initiative Trish said:-

'The Shrewsbury Circuit, through the ministry of the Church of the Good Shepherd, seeks to strengthen and maintain its links with its faithful membership when age or ill health prevent church attendance. By bringing the church to them in their homes, we continue to embrace them in the fellowship of the church and to accompany them on their spiritual journey.'

The silver-grey harvest field is a large and growing field in this country. Fresh expressions are needed for those of more mature years just as much as they are for any other demographic group.

Conclusion

It is too soon for conclusions. This book describes beginnings. The end is in the future. There can be no carefully worked out plan for the future. By the very nature of its material – fresh expressions – there cannot be.

There is evidence that the Methodist Church is capable of doing more than react to the emergence of fresh expressions. In districts, circuits, and local churches there are a large and growing number of people responding to the connexional priority of developing fresh ways of being church. Vision is developing, initiative is being taken, resources are being released and new ministries are being discovered.
To make the most of the opportunity afforded by this move of God's Spirit we must be prepared to bless what is happening. The emergence of fresh expressions of church in the early 21st century does, however, raise issues, which are challenging. In adapting our missiological thinking to the 21st century British context, we may find ourselves rethinking both our ecclesiology and our structures.

On the first Fresh Expressions DVD Ashley Cooper said of Taste and See *'God is calling us on a journey. We don't know where we are heading but we know we're heading with him …*
If you ask me where we will be in twelve months time the honest answer is 'I don't know'. We're on a sharp learning curve, we feel we're on a roller-coaster ride and God is just taking us. All we are trying to be is obedient to what God is calling us to do and that is a very exciting but scary place to be.'
We would echo this.

As a final thought provoking piece we offer an article by Tom Stuckey. At the end of his year as President he spoke to Conference. He has amended his address for publication here. You may not agree with him, but he will set you thinking.

Questions

Read this final article carefully, make notes as you do so.
- **What do you think of the signs Tom describes in section 1?**
- **What do you think of the three parts of Tom's 'mixed economy' model (Section 2)**
- **What would you add to or take away from Tom's list of necessary changes? (section 3)**

If you are studying this book as a group you might read the article as 'homework' and bring your conclusions together for discussion.

The Time is Short

Tom Stuckey

(Amended form of the Address given by the President at the Ministerial Session of Conference 2006)

My Conference Address at Torquay focused on the twin themes of 'theology' and 'the person of the Holy Spirit'. That address finished with the wave-beat of the sea; the gentle caress of the Spirit. Let's start where I left off. Jesus walks beside the sea and calls disciples after he has announced 'The time is fulfilled, and the kingdom of heaven is at hand; repent and believe in the Gospel'. (Mark 1:15-16).

There are two Greek words for 'time', chronos and kairos. The first word is clock-time measured by chronometers, the second relates to that moment when linear time and eternity are encapsulated in a single elective moment of opportunity. Unless an immediate response is made, God's kairos passes.

Methodism is approaching a kairos moment; a brief window of opportunity, possibly only five years at the most, in which to turn the Church around, or to be more accurate 'to repent and believe'. To repent is another way of saying we face reality and change decisively. To believe is another way of saying we must trust God and risk all. The kairos moment is now. What leads me to say this?

Part 1 - reading the signs

1. We are destroying the very planet which sustains our life

The four horseman of the apocalypse are already galloping across our planet leaving trails of destruction in their wake. The white horse of imperialism - some would say American globalisation; the fiery red horse of military invasion and terrorist atrocity; the black horse of plague famine and natural disaster and finally the pale horse of death – death from the carbon emissions which blot out the sun.

I explained in my book *Into the Far Country* that the rainbow covenant established through Noah is the foundational covenant of mission. This puts humanity's responsibility for the planet on the mission agenda. Christians must link hands with people of good-will, regardless of religion or race, in a global mission to save the planet. The time is short. We must repent and believe!

2. The violent clash of cultures

In his book *Apocalypse Now*, Duncan Forester tells how, when he heard the news of the destruction of the twin towers on 9/11, he opened his Bible and read Mark 13. He suggests we no longer stand optimistically at the end of history but have entered an age of terror where 'Apocalyptic theology' becomes an essential theological key for understanding the truth behind events. We may be facing a new 'Dark Age' of fanatical religious conflicts. Are we theologically equipped? The Church must quickly jettison surplus baggage, recover essential gospel priorities and assume flexible forms to survive in such a time as this. We must repent and believe!

3. The shifting centre of Christianity

Almost 60% of Christians live in Africa, Asia, Latin America and the Pacific. Pentecostal growth has transformed the global Christian landscape. The era of Western liberal Christianity is passing and the day of Southern conservative Christianity has dawned. We have to wrestle not just with theological diversity but with a possible collision between liberal and conservative theologies. The future of the rich Western Church lies in becoming a receiving Church in which we allow the fast growing conservative churches of the poor to challenge our culture, our wealth, our traditional superiority, our complacency and the liberal nature of our Christianity. Can we contemplate such a challenge as gift? We must repent and believe!

4. The rising Spirit within our own culture

The prophets of the 60s predicted the demise of religion as the God of the gaps was pushed out. This has not happened; instead religion is enjoying a remarkable renaissance. The process of secularization has 'de-regulated' religion. In our contemporary narcissistic culture of choice, DIY spirituality, virtual reality, fantasy, magic and dark superstition reign. Outsiders are not looking to the institutional Church for their religion. Can the Church plant itself in this new culture? We must repent and believe! We must change and take risks.

5. The edge of Pentecost

God's Spirit blows in waves of grace and has been doing so throughout history as peoples, nations and communities are given their own kairos moment. Is this moment now approaching us in Britain? For years we have lived with decline and accepted it as the norm. What if the wind of the Spirit is starting to blow over our dry bones? In my preaching around the Connexion I have become more and more aware of desperate hunger for the Word of God. What if the shortage of ministers is God's vehicle for breaking the cycle of parental dependency which exists between some ministers and churches? Could our decline be the work of God as he breaks us down in order to lead us to true repentance and faith?

What is the Spirit saying to us? I believe God is saying we stand on the edge of Pentecost and that church growth is possible. According to Orlando Costas there are four features:
- 'numerical' growth,
- 'organic' growth where the organisation and structure becomes fluid and flexible enough to take account of the Church's context and the movement of the Spirit,
- 'conceptual' growth. If there is no theological, emotional and spiritual development then despite numerical increase, the Church is not growing,
- 'incarnational' growth. This relates to the degree in which the Church is prophetically participating in the afflictions of the world through prayer, action and identification with the powerless and marginalized.

'The time is fulfilled, and the kingdom of heaven is at hand; repent and believe in the Gospel.'

Part 2 - the church reshaped

John Hull in his theological critique of *Mission-shaped Church* reminds us of a splendid sentence. 'Start with the Church and the mission will probably get lost. Start with mission and it is likely that the Church will be found'.

There is a brief opportunity for traditional church as the last baby boomer generation who attended Sunday School become senior citizens. Some of these will look to traditional church. After that the only advance will come from cross-cultural evangelism.

We have reached the end of 'generational' growth whereby children of Christian parents, through the processes of Baptism, Sunday School, and Confirmation become future members of the Church. A seismic cultural shift has taken place leaving three generations out of touch with Christian culture and tradition. Further, those seeking God are no longer prepared to fight their way through what they regard as a jungle of obsolete ecclesiastical baggage to enter a church building which has all the features of a heritage site housing a nostalgic community.

Making new Christians has to be the principle aim and 'fresh expressions' a way of achieving it. Nevertheless as the apocalyptic symptoms of violence increase some outsiders, seeking refuge, may turn to some traditional forms of church (for example the cathedrals). We have to evolve a 'mixed economy' Church. 'Fresh expressions', which are multiplying at an encouraging rate, provide a hopeful counterpoint to the decline of traditional church. In future there will be far fewer church buildings and a greater use made of renting secular properties.

Some 'fresh expressions' as described in *Mission-shaped Church* look like the offspring of traditional church who, like the children of an aging parents still carrying the powerful genes of past ideas of church. While some 'fresh expressions' are very imaginative others do little more than exchange the organ for the piano, or use PowerPoint instead of hymn books believing this will make a significant difference. Many 'fresh expressions' are not radical enough since they do not adequately express 'kingdom theology' which is essential if we are in the business of changing the world and not simply preserving the Church.

I believe we must explore a third theologically adventuresome alternative which I shall label 'emerged church'. I suggested in my book *Into the Far Country* that such communities are neither planted nor the product of 'pioneer' ministry. They are kingdom communities springing from the soil of some particular need beyond the borders of church. They are fluid, inclusive and transient. Such 'churches' pose difficult theological questions and raise acute issues of oversight. We have few people, either lay or ordained, who have the necessary gifts or are suitable training to work with such radical forms of church. What 'emerged' churches require is a 'theological consultant' rather than a pioneer minister or leader.

A 'mixed economy' Church will have main three models.
- Traditional church, re-modelled, opened up, user friendly with worship which is vibrant and relevant to those attending.
- Fresh expressions, sometimes meeting on church premises and sometimes not; certainly not tied to Sunday for worship. The result of 'pioneering ministries'

- Emerged church, transient, springing up through the Spirit and requiring very special gifts of ministry.

What I am suggesting is not new. The first two models were embraced by the first Methodists who attended the parish church and the Methodist Society. The last model was advocated in the 60s but suffered from a secular-ized theology. Then along came charismatic movement bringing a renewal of worship. What I am seeking is a theological synthesis. Our contemporary culture is very different from the 60s. It is not longer optimistic; it is more diverse, plural and violent. We failed to seize opportunities in the past; will it be any different now that God's judgement is falling more heavily upon the Church?

Now is the time when we must repent which is another way of saying we must face reality and change decisively. Now is the time when we must 'believe' which is another way of saying we must trust God and risk all.

Part 3 - necessary changes

If we are not to miss the kairos moment what must be done? In my travels I have repeatedly encountered the following:

- Ministers burdened by the connexional obsession with 'form filling',
- The resistance of congregations to change and their blindness to the bigger picture,
- Ministers and superintendents bogged down in maintenance models of ministry,
- The unwillingness or inability of many of our ordained ministers to work in a team with each other and with lay people,
- Frustrated persons (ministers and lay people) who have the vision and gifts to make a difference but who are not given the opportunity to exercise them.

I list some immediate tasks.

1. Focus leadership
Encourage diversity across the Connexion but also focus leadership clearly in the persons of the Presidency team (both present, ex and past), the General Secretary, (for Conference) and district chairs (for synod). Some of these should be bishops. The Connexional Team to relinquish what is perceived in many places to be centralizing control and become more clearly a servicing agency for Conference, districts and circuits. Bishops should be apostolic church planters like the Celtic bishops.

2. Recruit younger presbyters and deacons for 'pioneer ministry'

3. Quickly ordain and licence 100 local preachers to the non-stipendiary ministry of word and sacrament
Let the district licence them to exercise pastoral charge and provide a maintenance ministry and terminal care or some of our traditional churches.

4. Head-hunt presbyters/deacons/lay workers who can work with emerged churches
Head-hunt those persons who have the necessary gifts and track record. There must be practical evidence that they can do this. Some ministers think they can but it is more in their imagination than in reality. Such presbyters among them should be stationed outside of the normal matching process. Because such evangelist persons are often individualists we must ensure a system of oversight which provides mentoring, peer learning and mutual accountability.

5. Shift the balance of training from initial to continuing development
Because the suggestions above confront traditional assumptions that all ministers should be trained at the same level we must approach the issue of competency differently. An annual appraisal system should be linked with a personal development plan and a training programme. Every presbyter, deacon and lay worker should be required to attend courses to maintain their licence or right to minister. The balance of training should be shifted from initial to on-going.

6. Ensure that those with evangelistic gifts in circuits are released

Ensure that in specified circuits within a district at least one member of staff, presbyter, deacon or lay-worker, who having the gift of an evangelist, is released from pastoral charge and given responsibility for generating a 'fresh expression' of church.

7. Shift power from local church to circuit and district

Provide enabling action to shift power from the local church to the circuit meeting and district as primary resourcing units, giving them legal authority to close resistant churches, and sell burdensome buildings.

Part 4 - postscript

We stand poised on the edge of sparkling possibilities, but the time is short and we have to cast our nets on the other side. We must change direction, act decisively and risk all. That is what repentance and faith is about. Jesus says, 'The time is fulfilled, and the kingdom of heaven is at hand; repent and believe in the Gospel' He then walks beside the silver sea. So must we.

'Methodism is a classic example of a renewal movement within Christianity, a fresh expression of Christianity which was frozen out by the rigidity of ecclesiastical structures and the unbendingness of tradition. Their enthusiasm reflected the earliest post-Pentecost enthusiasm of the first believers. Their sense of intimacy with Christ was a trait they learned from the Moravians. The experience of assurance, of assurance as a feeling and not just a conviction is imprinted on their hymns. Disowned by the established Church they found a reality and vitality of church in their home-based 'societies'; they rediscovered the house church. And their insistence that there should be no order of priesthood distinct from the priestly ministry of the whole people of God encouraged a growth and diversity of ministry which brought the gospel to generations overlooked by those who insisted on traditional forms and hierarchy. Methodism reminds us that fresh expressions are not only the way in which Christianity began but also the way in which Christianity will be revived.'

Jimmy Dunn, Methodist local preacher, former Professor of New Testament, Durham University.
[From a lecture given at Durham 26 April 2007]

Britain in the 21st century is a society of unparalleled diversity. In recent decades Conference has consistently responded to the changing nature of British society. The *Our Calling* process adopted by Conference in 2000 developed five *Priorities* adopted by Conference in 2004. Among these is 'Encouraging fresh ways of being Church'.

Our Covenant partner, the Church of England, has also been responding to the changing environment of our mission. The Fresh Expressions initiative is a response to the Anglican report *Mission-shaped Church*. Graham Horsley, Secretary for Church Planting and Evangelism was involved in writing this report.

Recent Presidents of Conference have called the Church to rediscover the way God's Spirit initiates fresh expressions of church. Tom Stuckey made the Church aware of the need for fresh expressions of church. Graham Carter has emphasised our call to discipleship, something fundamental to all expressions of church, fresh or otherwise.

In 2006 Conference directed that a report be brought about connexional strategy with '11 to 25 year olds and the missing generation'[35] There is interest in spirituality among this 'missing generation'.

Conference 1987 – Home Mission Report

'there are a number of communities within British society which have proved particularly resistant to the ministry of traditional churches. Some of these communities are defined geographically… and others are defined culturally, ethnically, or in terms of people's work or life-style. Wherever there are communities whose members are noticeably under-represented in our churches, then there is a prime facie case for considering new forms of local congregational life.'

Conference 1999
– Called to Love and Praise - took a good look at Methodist ecclesiology in the light of changes in society.
– Flexible Patterns of Ministry

[35] 8/51/1 **Additional Appendix 1A** *(continued)* Memorial 11 (2004) - *Connexional Team Strategy: Towards a renewed vision for work with children and young people*

Conference 2000
– *Our Calling* adopted
– *The Role and Recognition of Evangelists*

Conference 2002
– *Evangelism and Evangelists in the Methodist Church*
'The Methodist Church at the beginning of the 21st century faces a situation different from that during most of its history. Society has changed, and the predominant culture is now a secularised, post-modern and post-Christian one in which we can no longer assume that people have any basic Christian knowledge or understanding. If the need in earlier years was to call people back to faith, the need today is for forms of primary evangelism which assume nothing.'

Recommendations:
Circuits are encouraged to consider appointing evangelists to work with those outside the activities of their existing churches and to consider the planting of new forms of church to meet those people's spiritual needs.

Conference 2004
– adopted five *Priorities* in the *Our Calling* process including 'developing fresh ways of being Church'.

Conference 2006
– Diaconal Ministry: response to Notice of Motion 5 (2004) noted the place the diaconate is called to play in the development of fresh ways of being church. Conference noted the distinctive contribution of the Methodist Diaconal Order to the whole Church and notes that 'encouraging fresh expressions of church' mirrors the vision that gave rise to the order in the late 19th century.

Appendix - Resources

from

Courses and events

- In partnership with others, we have developed training materials for one-day events and short courses that are now being used more widely through the network of associate missioners.

- **Strategic conferences**

    for districts and dioceses to explore the vision. Examples include a joint synod in the London NE district and St Albans Diocese, a joint Diocesan and District conference for 200 in West Yorkshire and a day for 600 people in Norwich Cathedral, The team have visited about two thirds of the Methodist districts and almost every diocese. Some districts have picked up the fresh expressions theme through local staff.

- **Training courses**

  o Vision Days – one day courses presented for a grouping of circuits or deaneries and their ecumenical partners. Vision Days can be presented at district level.

The largest Vision Day so far was an ecumenical day in Lincoln Cathedral in April 2007. The smallest, in Jersey, had 25 people.

  o **Mission Shaped Intro** – changing minds, changing church – a six evening course over six weeks. Run this one yourselves at local level. Available September 2007

  o **Mission shaped ministry** – A one year course aimed at people wanting to develop, or involved in developing, a fresh expression of church. Also very helpful to people who are 'gatekeepers', who can give permission and encouragement to others. Normally one residential w/e, two/three Saturdays and eight monthly evenings. Other formats possible. Fresh Expressions hopes to make sure this is available within one hour travelling for 90% of the British population. For details see the Fresh expressions website.

Publications

- Simple and accessible for church councils and small groups:
o *Moving on in a Mission-shaped Church* was published in September 2005 and sold 15,000 copies in three months.
o *Starting a Fresh Expression* published early 2006.
o *Listening for Mission* in October 2006. Two more booklets in the same series are planned.
- **Expressions: the DVD,** stories of church for a changing culture. The DVD features 14 stories of fresh expressions from across the country. Presented by Dianne Louise Jordan. Sold 1,500 copies in its first two weeks of release.
- **Expressions: the DVD 2:** Changing Church in Every Place. Four 20 minute programmes featuring stories of fresh expressions. Six five-minute discussion starters. Presented by Dianne Louise Jordan.
- **Expressions: the newspaper:** 30,000 copies were distributed free of charge between November and January. A second edition was published for Methodist Conference in Edinburgh. The third edition published in February 2007 is out of stock and being reprinted.

Web based information sharing

- **www.freshexpressions.org.uk** (website) a source of basic information and help. The site receives thousands of visits each month.
- **www.freshexpressions.info** a web database, available to organizations working in supporting and developing fresh expressions of church, which will enable coordination of training, events and fresh expressions.
- **'Share'** - the on-line guide (Coming soon)

The wisdom needed for fresh expressions of church is currently being learned in a thousand or more different places. Although each fresh expression is different, some common lessons, mistakes and principles are already emerging and more will do so in the future. A vital part of supporting growth in fresh expressions of church is therefore to collect what is being learned in one place and enable practitioners to connect to this growing body of wisdom.

To meet this need the team is developing an 'on-line guide' that will play a key role in the provision of learning materials and distilled practical wisdom that will be essential for all of this training provision. We are currently working with a small number of national agencies or institutions to partner with us in the development of the on-line guide and, together, to sustain it beyond 2009.

Other Resources

Mission-shaped Church:
Church planting and fresh expressions of church in a changing context ISBN No: 0715140132, Church House Publishing 2004, £10.95
This report is essential reading. The Report to the General Synod of the Church of England which marked the recognition of that denomination of the need to encourage fresh expressions. Among the working group who produced this book was Graham Horsley, Methodist Connexional Evangelism Policy and Church Planting Secretary.
Download from: **http://www.cofe. anglican.org/info/papers/mission_ shaped_church.pdf**
Glasson, Barbara, **Mixed Up Blessing**, Inspire, Peterborough
Stuckey, Tom, **Beyond the Box**, Inspire, Peterborough
Atkins, Martyn D, **Preaching in a Cultural Context**, Foundery Press

Allen, Roland, **Missionary methods – St Paul's or Ours,** Eerdmans/ Paternoster
Allen, Roland, **The Spontaneous Expansion of the Church http://www.gospeltruth.net/allen/ spon_expanofch.htm**
Allen was an Anglican missionary to China at the time of the Boxer rebellion, at the turn of the 19th century. His thoughts on mission were fifty years ahead of his time and still challenging today.
Donovan, Vincent, **Christianity Rediscovered**, Orbis, New York
Donavan, the 'apostle to the Masai' was a Roman Catholic missionary who, having admitted to his failure to reach the Masai through traditional methods was introduced to the writings of Roland Allen....
Bosch, David, **Transforming Mission,** Orbis, New York
A big read! Probably the most significant work on missiology in the late 20th century.
Newbigin, Lesslie, **The Gospel in a Pluralist Society**, SPCK

Books from Church House Publishing
– All written from an Anglican perspective.
Ed. Croft, Steven, **The Future of the Parish System,**

An interesting book with contributions from Archbishop Rowan Williams and others. (What might a 'The Future of the Circuit System' book look like?)
In the mission-shaped series.
Withers, Margaret, **Mission Shaped Children**
Gaze, Sally, **Mission Shaped and Rural**
Bayes, Paul and Sledge, Tim and others, **Mission-shaped Parish**
Hope, Susan, **Mission-shaped Spirituality**
Sudworth, Tim, Cray, Graham, Russell, Chris, **Mission-shaped Youth**
Encounters on the Edge, a series of research papers from the Church Army's Sheffield Centre, Wilson Carlile Campus, Sheffield S3 7RZ
www.encountersontheedge.org.uk

Books on Cell Church and other small group ways of being church:
Resurrecting the Classes – an introduction to Cell Church for Methodists. Available from the Secretary for Evangelism and Church Planting, MCH, 25 Marylebone Road, NW1 5JR
Astin, Howard, **Body and Cell**, Monarch
Cell UK Magazine and website
www.celluk.co.uk
See also David Lowes Watson's books on Covenant Discipleship c.f.
http://www.gbod.org/smallgroup/cd/

Some resources that can help with fresh expression for older people: Church Army Research papers
- No. 1 Taking the church into residential care homes in Eastbourne.
- No. 2 St. Stephen's Seniors: Christ to the Elderly and Lonely in East Twickenham
- No. 3 PSALM Project for Seniors And Lifelong Ministry
- No. 4 The Outlook Trust: Christian Hope and Encouragement for Older People.
- No. 5 'Holiday at Home' Running events for older people during the summer holidays.

Available from the Sheffield Centre, Church Army' Research Unit. Email l.keith@sheffieldcentre.org.uk
Tel. 0114 272 7451

- **www.freshexpressions.org.uk**
- **www.encountersontheedge.org.uk**
- **www.churcharmy.org.uk**
- **www.levesoncentre.org.uk**
- **www.outlook-trust.org.uk**
- **www.valuingolderexperience.org**
- **www.parche.org.uk**

The Internet:
. . . .

There is a host of material on
the internet. A search on 'fresh
expressions' or 'emerging church'
on a search engine will list thousands of sites.
We recommend that readers should
first go to the Fresh expressions
website **www.freshexpressions.org.
uk** and then follow the links under
'training and resources'.

About the authors:

Pete Pillinger was born in Sussex. On leaving school he worked in the pharmaceutical industry and Health Service before becoming a Methodist minister. In his 28 years as a minister he has served in Cornwall, Sri Lanka, Brixton and Lincolnshire. Whilst in Lincolnshire he was involved in the development of a Cell Church and also in running a multimedia café church. He is currently a member of the Methodist Church Connexional Team and seconded to Fresh Expressions. He is married to Helen and has three grown up children. When not doing ministry related things Pete loves to walk mountains – not something there is much opportunity for in Lincolnshire.

Andrew Roberts is a Methodist minister based in the West Midlands. Married to Shona they have one son, Matthew. After graduating with a degree in economics, Andrew worked for Ford Motor Company as a financial analyst. He was one of the founder students of the Wesley Study Centre in Durham and has served in circuit appointments in Doncaster and the Stourbridge and Brierley Hill Circuits. After working as a Director of the Saltmine Trust he took up his present appointments. He now serves the Wolverhampton and Shrewsbury as Mission Enabler and the Fresh Expressions Team in which he has responsibilities for Discipleship and Vision Days. Andrew achieved his fifteen minutes of fame when he was the headline act in Clergy on the Catwalk. Away from work he has a passion for motorsport and an irrational interest in Aston Villa.

Pete and Andrew are grateful to the many people who have collaborated in the production of this resource.